# Mongolia

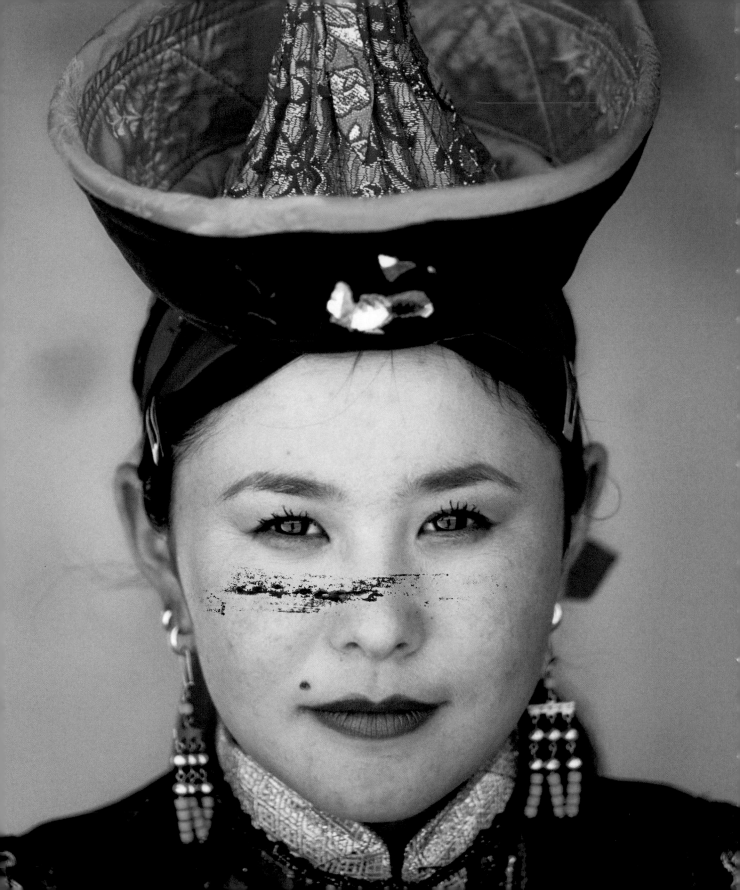

# Mongolia

## Withdrawn

BY ALLISON LASSIEUR

*Enchantment of the World*
*Second Series*

Children's Press®

*A Division of Scholastic Inc.*

NEW YORK   TORONTO   LONDON   AUCKLAND   SYDNEY
MEXICO CITY   NEW DELHI   HONG KONG
DANBURY, CONNECTICUT

**Frontispiece:** A Mongolian dancer

*Consultant:* Bolortsetseg Smith, Instructor, Center for East Asian Studies,
        Western Washington University, Bellingham, Washington.

*Please note: All statistics are as up-to-date as possible at the time of publication.*

Book production by Herman Adler

Library of Congress Cataloging-in-Publication Data

Lassieur, Allison.
  Mongolia / By Allison Lassieur.
    p. cm. — (Enchantment of the world. Second series)
  Includes bibliographical references and index.
  ISBN-13: 978-0-516-24903-2
  ISBN-10: 0-516-24903-7
  1. Mongolia—Juvenile literature. I. Title. II. Series.
  DS798.L295 2007
  951.7'3—dc22                        2006017143

# Mongolia

**Cover photo:**
Herder on
horseback

# Contents

Camels in the Gobi

Traditional singers

# The Mystery of Mongolia

EW PLACES ON EARTH SEEM AS REMOTE AND UNKNOWN AS Mongolia. To go to "Outer Mongolia" is to be in the middle of nowhere. Until the nineteenth century, few Europeans had ever been there. Those who had brought back descriptions of a land and people that were so fantastic that few believed them.

A young Italian man named Marco Polo traveled to Mongolia in the thirteenth century. He was the first European to describe the Mongol civilization. His book, *The Travels of Marco Polo*, caused a sensation. Europeans simply didn't believe that an empire—one that was richer, more powerful, and in many ways more civilized than their own world—could exist there. Even today, there is controversy as to whether Marco Polo really saw the fantastic things he described.

*Opposite:* **Mongolia is the least crowded country on earth.**

**Khublai Khan sits on a throne in this sixteenth-century illustration from *The Book of Marvels of Marco Polo*.**

Lake Baikal

RUSSIA

Turta

Uvs Nuur

Hatgal   Khövsgöl Nuur

Ölgii   Ulaangom   Sükhbaatar

Khovd   Mörön   Darkhan

Ugtam Uul Nat. Rés.   Dagurian S.P.A.

Onon-Balj Nat'l Con. Park   Ereentsav

Onon   Yakhi Lake Nat. Rés.   Nömrög S.P.A.

Selenge R.   Erdenet   Khan Khentii S.P.A.   Choibalsan

Uliastai   Bulgan   Ulaanbaatar   Kherlen R.

Tsetserleg   Hadasan   Toson Khulstai Nature Reserve

Tsagaan-Olom   Khustai Nat'l Con. Park   Khar Yamaat Nat. Rés.   Eastern Steppe S.P.A.

Altai   Baruun-Urt   Lkhachinvandad Uul Nature Reserve

Bayankhongor   Arvaikheer   Gun-Galuut Nature Reserve

Mandalgovi   Buyant   Ganga Lake Natural Mon.

Great Gobi Strictly Protected Area   Gurvansaikan Nat'l Con. Park   Boroyn Tal

Dalanzadgad

N
W   E
S

CHINA

**Mongolia**

## "I Have Not Told Half of What I Saw!"

Traveling to Mongolia was the trip of a lifetime for seventeen-year-old Marco Polo. His father, Niccolò, and his uncle, Maffeo, both merchants, had already traveled to the court of the great Mongol leader Khublai Khan when Marco was a small boy. When they decided to return in 1271, they took an excited Marco with them. It would prove to be a decision that would change Europe.

It took the Polos three and a half years to travel to the Mongol's capital city of Khanbaliq (the name means "Great Residence of the Khan," or king), which is now the city of Beijing, China. During the trip, Marco grew from a gangly teenager to a confident man of twenty-one. Khublai Khan knew they were coming. Forty days before they arrived, he sent a royal escort to accompany them.

What Marco Polo didn't know as he rode with the royal escort was that the Mongols controlled a vast empire that stretched across 11 million to 12 million square miles (28 million to 31 million square kilometers). Khublai Khan, who

Art, science, and foreign trade flourished under the rule of Khublai Khan.

was born in 1215, was the grandson of the first great Mongol leader, Genghis Khan. Khublai had conquered China, adding it to the Mongol empire, which included the lands from present-day China to the Caspian Sea, a huge lake that lies between Asia and Europe. Khublai Khan assumed the throne in 1260 and founded the Mongol capital in 1263.

Marco, who had a gift for languages and diplomacy, became a favorite of Khublai Khan. He had a chance to see and describe many of the wonders of the Mongol culture of the time. He was especially enthralled by the khan's summer palace, which he called the "greatest palace that ever was." The walls and ceilings were covered with gold and silver. Sculptures of dragons, beasts, and birds decorated the walls. He told of buildings colored in yellow, red, green, and blue that shone like crystal. The palace had one room so large that six thousand people could dine in it. Marco described other marvels of the Mongols, including paper money and a strange rock that could burn like wood. The rock was coal, which was unknown in Europe at the time.

It was seventeen years before Marco Polo returned to Italy, never to see the Mongol empire or the great Khublai Khan again. He became a sensation after his book was published in Europe. People could not believe his tales of a Mongol culture that was so rich and refined. Even when Marco was on his deathbed, people still doubted his story. In 1324, as Marco lay dying, a priest begged him to confess that his stories were all lies. Marco refused, saying, "I have not told half of what I saw!"

## Mongolia Today

Mongolia today is still unknown to the rest of the world in many ways. Slowly, however, it is opening up to curious travelers and international business. Modern-day visitors find a people who deeply respect their ancient tradition, while eagerly embracing the future.

A growing number of visitors are traveling to Mongolia to experience its sweeping scenery. In 2002, tourism brought $103 million into the Mongolian economy.

# Mountain, Steppe, and Desert

MONGOLIA IS SANDWICHED BETWEEN TWO POWERFUL countries: Russia to the north and China to the south. Though Mongolia is located between these two enormous countries, it has remained isolated for most of its history.

The main feature of Mongolia is its endless miles of wide-open, level land called steppes. Mongolia has the world's lowest population density, with only four people per square

*Opposite:* **Camels graze near sand dunes in the Gobi Desert.**

**Car tires dig easily into the dry Mongolian steppes.**

mile (two per sq km). It has enormous areas of land unspoiled by fences, roads, or large cities. The different regions of Mongolia have a rich variety of ecosystems that support plentiful wildlife and natural resources. Many people consider Mongolia to be the last unspoiled Asian country.

Some travelers to Mongolia imagine riding horseback from one end of the country to the other. They dream of riding through its pristine landscape past breathtakingly beautiful mountains. While this romantic dream can be a reality, Mongolia is also harsh and unforgiving. Extreme temperatures, extreme geography, and sometimes extreme isolation make Mongolia a difficult, though rewarding, country to explore.

A group of Korean tourists ride horses in Mongolia. Much of Mongolia is open land with no fences, so it is ideal for riding horses.

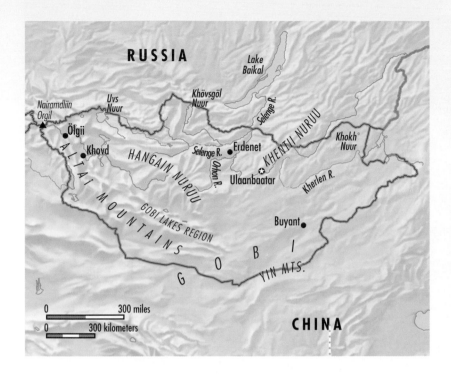

## Mongolia's Geographic Features

**Area:** 603,909 square miles (1,564,116 sq km)

**Highest Elevation:** Nairamdliin Orgil, 14,350 feet (4,374 m)

**Lowest Elevation:** Khokh Nuur, 1,699 feet (518 m)

**Largest Lake:** Uvs Nuur, 1,293 square miles (3,350 sq km)

**Largest River:** Orkhon River, 698 miles (1,124 km)

**Largest City:** Ulaanbaatar, 850,000

**Average High Temperature in Ulaanbaatar:**
January 2°F (-19°C)
July 72°F (22°C)

**Average Annual Precipitation:** 8–9 inches (20–22 cm)

### Measuring Mongolia

Mongolia is a landlocked country—it borders neither an ocean nor a sea. Stretching across 603,909 square miles (1,564,116 sq km), it is twice the size of Texas and only slightly smaller than Alaska. At times during its history, Mongolia was even bigger. A large section of Siberia, which is now part of Russia, was once part of Mongolia. The area of China now known as Inner Mongolia was also once part of the great Mongol empire.

The majestic Altai Mountains rise in western Mongolia. They are filled with jagged peaks and rushing rivers.

## Mountains

Mongolia boasts three major mountain ranges. The Altai Mountains, which are in the southwestern area of the country, are the highest. The highest point in Mongolia, a mountain peak called Nairamdliin Orgil ("Mount Friendship") is part of this mountain range. Nairamdliin Orgil lies in the extreme western part of the country, in the area where Mongolia, China, and Russia meet. The Altai Mountains are breathtaking, with snowcapped mountains and icy glaciers. Between the mountain peaks lie desert areas where rain rarely falls.

The Hangai Nuruu occupy much of central and north-central Mongolia. These mountains are lower and older than the Altai range. Some parts of the Hangai are forested, and others have beautiful alpine pastures. Deep in the northern slope of the Hangai is the source of the Selenge River. The Selenge is Mongolia's largest river in terms of the amount of water it carries, but another river, the Kherlen, is the country's longest.

The Khentii Nuruu range dominates eastern Mongolia. These mountains are popular with tourists and hikers, who love to explore the beautiful rivers, forests, and climbable peaks. This range is also conveniently located near the capital city of Ulaanbaatar.

A river cuts through the rugged mountains in western Mongolia. Trees grow only along the riverbank because everywhere else is too dry.

## Lakes

Mongolia has many freshwater and saltwater lakes. The most popular lake for recreation is Khövsgöl Nuur, the second-oldest lake in the world. It contains 2 percent of the world's supply of freshwater. The land around the lake is magnificent, filled with pristine forests and mountain peaks. Tourists enjoy swimming, fishing, hiking, camping, and bird-watching along Khövsgöl Nuur.

The largest lake in Mongolia is Uvs Nuur. It is a low-lying, saltwater lake in northwest Mongolia, near the Russian border.

**The deep, clear Khövsgöl Nuur is one of Mongolia's natural treasures. Ninety-six rivers flow out of the lake.**

The Mongolian steppes are vast and empty. They provide the perfect habitat for gazelles, migrating birds, and many other creatures.

## Steppes

A steppe is a large, grassy plain without trees. Steppes can be semidesert, or they can be covered with grasses and shrubs. Steppes have a unique climate. They are too dry to support a forest, but too moist to turn to desert. Steppes usually have hot summers and cold winters.

Mongolia is famous for its steppes. The endless miles of grassland cover most of eastern Mongolia and extend all the way to the western regions. Mongolia's eastern steppes form the largest expanse of unspoiled grassland in the world. No fences break up this vast sea of knee-high grass that covers nearly 96,500 square miles (250,000 sq km). People from around the world travel to Mongolia to experience its quiet isolation.

Sheep graze on the steppes. Nomads have been herding animals on the steppes for thousands of years.

At first glance, the steppes might seem empty of people and animals. But that is not the case. Nomads use most of the area to graze their livestock. More than thirty million sheep, horses, goats, cows, and camels are raised in Mongolia.

The steppes have begun to feel the pressure of overgrazing. In 1990, Mongolia was facing swift political and economic changes. Many families faced an uncertain future in cities and villages. Some decided to return to the nomadic lifestyle and began herding again. This caused a huge increase in the number of animals that relied on the grasslands for survival. In some areas, overgrazing is becoming an environmental issue. Many areas are now becoming trampled by livestock and compacted by off-road vehicles.

## Looking at Mongolia's Cities

Mongolia's capital of Ulaanbaatar is by far the largest city in the country. But some of the nation's smaller cities are also noteworthy.

Ölgii (below) is located in northwestern Mongolia at an elevation of 5,610 feet (1,710 meters). Its 28,500 people are predominantly of Kazakh ethnicity. The Kazakhs were traditionally a nomadic people. They have lived in central Asia for more than four hundred years. They first started to visit Mongolia from their native Kazakhstan in the 1840s to graze their sheep in the mountains during summer. In winter, they would return to their native lands. Eventually, many Kazakhs settled in Mongolia.

Most residents of Ölgii are Muslims, followers of the religion of Islam. One of the city's main features is a mosque, a Muslim house of worship, that is home to the Islamic Center of Mongolia.

Most of the buildings in Ölgii are square, concrete structures. In several areas surrounding the city, people live in gers, traditional Mongolian circular huts. The Altai Mountains rise above Ölgii, giving the townspeople dramatic views. Many tourists use Ölgii as a rest stop before tackling the Altai Mountains.

Khovd (above), with a population of 31,000, is the largest city in western Mongolia. It was once a military outpost for the Manchu, a group that took over China in the seventeenth century. The Manchu maintained control of the city until 1912.

In the years since, Khovd has kept its Manchurian atmosphere while growing into a friendly, pleasant city. The Buyant River flows through Khovd. The city is fairly modern for Mongolia, with an agricultural institute and a university. The city's economy is mostly agricultural, but it also has a few industries including food processing and manufacturing building materials.

On the northern end of Khovd are the ruins of a huge walled compound that dates from 1762 and was built by Manchurian warlords. The compound once included temples, a graveyard, and the grand homes of the rulers who lived there. Today, all that remains are the ruined walls.

## The Gobi Desert

The Gobi Desert covers one-third of Mongolia and stretches into China. It is the fifth-largest desert in the world. In prehistoric times, the Gobi basin was part of a large inland sea. Today, it stretches almost 1,000 miles (1,600 km) east to west and 600 miles (1,000 km) north to south. The name *Gobi* comes from a Mongolian word that means "very large and dry."

Most people imagine the Gobi Desert as a vast area filled with sand dunes and hot wind. But sand dunes cover only about 3 percent of the Gobi. The desert is mostly huge areas of gravel and scrub plants. It is one of the least populated areas on earth, with only three people per square mile (one per sq km).

Camels are well-adapted to life in the desert. When they come across water, they can drink 30 gallons (135 liters) in less than fifteen minutes.

The Gobi is made up of several distinct ecological and geographic regions. Each region has its own unique characteristics. The eastern desert steppe includes the Yin Mountains and many low-lying areas with small ponds. To the west and southwest of this is the Alashan Plateau, a semidesert area. The plateau is surrounded by low mountains. Snowmelt from the mountains creates oases and areas of green. The Gobi Lakes valley is north of the Alashan Plateau. It includes sand dunes, lakes, and wetlands.

The Taklimakan desert region, which lies in both Mongolia and China, is the driest and warmest part of the Gobi. This region is located farther from the ocean than almost any other place on earth. The Taklimakan has the kind of landscape that comes to mind when people think of deserts. It is one of the world's largest shifting-sands deserts. More than 85 percent of the Taklimakan is filled with golden sand dunes, some can be 600 feet (200 m) high.

Gurvansaikhan National Park is in the Gobi Desert. It contains both craggy mountains and rippling sand dunes.

## A Harsh Climate

Mongolia is a land of extremes, and that includes its weather. The winters are long and cold, with temperatures sometimes dropping to −40 degrees Fahrenheit (−40 degrees Celsius). Temperatures stay below freezing in Ulaanbaatar for eight months of the year, and the ground in more than half the country is frozen year-round. Summers, particularly in the Gobi Desert, are scorching. During the height of summer—from June to August—temperatures can rise above 100°F (38°C).

Both summer and winter in Mongolia are dry. July and August are the wettest months, but the country averages only 8 to 9 inches (20 to 22 centimeters) of rain and snow throughout the year. In fact, most days, there is not even a cloud in the sky. Mongolia has an average of 257 cloudless days each year.

## The Future of Mongolia's Land

During much of the twentieth century, Mongolia was dependent on the Soviet Union, a huge country formed by Russia and some of its neighboring countries in the 1920s. The Soviets had a great deal of influence on Mongolia and brought factories, roads, mines, railroads, and power plants to the country.

In 1990, political change led the Soviets to leave Mongolia. They abandoned Mongolia's industries and ended the financial support that Mongolia had relied on. Mongolia has been searching for ways to support itself without that aid ever since. The easiest way to do that is to sell its natural resources. This has caused many people to be concerned that the unspoiled areas of Mongolia will one day be gone. For now, however, the march of progress is slow. The harsh beauty of the Mongolian landscape is safe for the time being.

A train carrying coal passes by a coal mine in Mongolia. Most of the nation's huge coal deposits have not yet been mined.

# Wild Mongolia

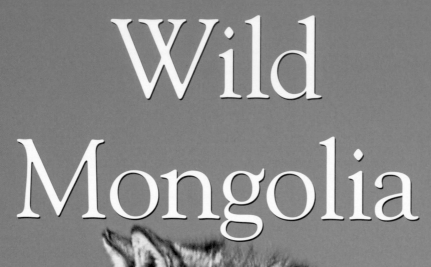

28

Mongolia has a striking variety of wildlife and plant life. It is home to 136 species of mammals, almost 400 species of birds, and 76 species of fish. Huge herds of gazelles thunder across the grassy steppes. Flocks of birds fly through the blue sky over lakes and rivers. Several endangered species hide in the forest and mountain areas. Though the Gobi Desert can appear barren, it too is home to a variety of animals and plants, many of them threatened or endangered.

In Mongolia, wild animals live side by side with domesticated animals such as horses, cattle, goats, sheep, and camels. Sometimes it is hard to tell which animals are wild and which are not, since they all share the vast Mongolian landscape.

*Opposite:* **Wolves are both feared and admired in Mongolia. According to legend, Mongolians are descended from a gray wolf.**

Brown bears are not always brown. They range in color from cream to brown to black.

## In the Forests and Mountains

The forests and mountains of Mongolia tend to have a cool climate, so the animals that live there must be able to thrive in cold weather. These areas are home to elk, deer, moose, wild boars, wolves, red foxes, wolverines, lynxes, brown bears, and small creatures such as rabbits and mice. Forest and mountain birds include woodpeckers, loons, and black kites, which are birds of prey related to the eagle.

Some animals that live in these colder areas of Mongolia are known for their rich furs. Sables, ermines, otters, and beavers were once plentiful in Mongolia's forests and mountains. Because they have long been hunted for their fur, they are now more rare. Muskrats, which are also hunted for their fur, were introduced into some parts of Mongolia and are now common.

Among the more unusual animals are great argali sheep. These wild sheep, which live high in the mountains, were first described by Marco Polo. Their huge, curling horns are prized by hunters, so these animals are in danger from hunting. They are also threatened by habitat loss, as herds of domestic sheep overgraze their feeding areas.

The great argali sheep and the Siberian ibex are among the largest wild animals in Mongolia. Although they are named for a part of Russia, Siberian ibex are common in high regions of Mongolia. They have huge, distinctive curved horns that attract hunters from around the world.

The musk deer is a shy member of the deer family that lives in mountain forests dominated by pine and fir. Although it is not an endangered species, these deer are threatened by hunting. They produce musk, a strong-smelling substance that

**Both male and female Siberian ibex have horns. The males' horns are bigger and have large bumps.**

is valuable as an ingredient in perfumes and cosmetics. Some people also think musk can improve health. One pound of the brown, waxy musk is worth more than US$25,000.

Larch, spruce, Siberian pine, birch, and fir dominate the forests and mountains of Mongolia. Most of the forests have a thick undergrowth of wildflowers and shrubs such as rhododendrons and azaleas. The forests are broken by meadows filled with grasses and flowers.

## Animals in Danger

Some animals face an uncertain future in Mongolia. The wild Bactrian camel is one of the world's rarest wild animals. Although millions of them live as domestic animals, just a few remain in the wild. In 2003, only 950 were reported in Mongolia and China. They now live in three small herds in the Gobi Desert. Bactrian camels are well suited to life in the harsh desert. They have thick eyelashes that protect their eyes from the stinging sands. Their slitlike nostrils can close to keep out sand and dust. Under the soles of their feet is a thick, hornlike layer that allows them to walk easily on hot sand or gravel. The Bactrian camel has become endangered because of hunting and because it now competes with domestic animals for pasture and water.

The long-eared jerboa lives in Mongolian desert areas. Though it stands and moves like a kangaroo, it is in fact a type of mouse. It has long hind legs, a long tail, and extremely big ears. Its powerful hind legs allow it to jump up to 10 feet (3 m) to escape predators. It uses its large ears to listen for the desert insects that it eats.

The Gobi bear is among the world's rarest animals. Only about 50 of these bears are left in the rocky, hilly areas of the Gobi Desert. They have suffered from competition with livestock and people for habitat, food, and water, and have been rare since the 1960s. Today, most Gobi bears live in strictly protected areas of the desert, which will hopefully keep them safe from people and habitat loss.

One of Mongolia's most elusive animals, the snow leopard, is also one of its rarest. Snow leopards live in the high mountains and are rarely seen. It is estimated that between 500 and 1,700 snow leopards still live in Mongolia. One reason for the snow leopard's decline has to do with the disappearance of its prey. Marmots, rodents that are the staple of a snow leopard's summer diet, are being heavily hunted by humans. Snow leopards themselves are also illegally hunted for their luxurious fur.

Pikas often carry leaves and grasses about. They store some of it to eat during the long winter.

## In the Steppes and Desert

The Mongolian steppes make a perfect home for herds of plant-eating creatures like gazelles. In the past, enormous herds of white-tail gazelles dominated the eastern Mongolian steppes. In the late 1960s, more than three hundred thousand gazelles roamed the area. In the Gobi Desert, black-tailed gazelles numbered about sixty thousand. Today, their numbers have plummeted because of habitat loss, hunting, and competition with domestic animals such as sheep and cattle. Although large herds of gazelles still live on the steppes and in desert areas, they are much smaller than they once were.

Other than gazelles, the only animals that are native to the steppes and desert areas are rodents. These include marmots, ground squirrels, and pikas. Pikas are part of the rabbit family and are also known as rock rabbits. In some places, they are called "whistling hares" because they make a high-pitched whistling sound when they are alarmed. The name *pika* comes

The Pallas's cat lives in the steppes. It comes out at night to hunt pikas and other rodents.

from the Russian word *pikat*, which means "to squeak." The desert steppes support other rodents such as hamsters, gerbils, and jerboas.

Predators roam Mongolia, including the small corsac fox. This reddish-gray fox has long legs, large ears, and a pointed snout. It can be found on the steppes and in semidesert areas of Mongolia. Corsac foxes live in burrows under the ground and hunt small animals such as birds, reptiles, and insects.

The Asiatic steppe cat looks like an ordinary house cat with a bushy tail that resembles a raccoon tail. These small predators prefer living in scrub or desert habitats where they can hunt for rodents and other small desert prey.

The steppe polecat isn't really a cat. Instead, it's related to weasels and ferrets. Steppe polecats dig burrows in the ground. They even make separate burrows for their food. When they are threatened, polecats spray their enemy with a strong, heavy scent.

The steppes and semideserts boast a variety of plants and vegetation. Grasses such as feather grass, June grass, ryegrass, wheatgrass, and fescue dominate the steppes. Scrubs, feather grasses, tumbleweed, and sagebrush can be found in the desert areas. Most of these plants are well suited to Mongolia's extreme temperatures and low rainfall.

Corsac foxes are more social than many foxes. They sometimes hunt in packs.

A ruddy shelduck leads its ducklings across a meadow in the Gobi. Shelducks are hardy and can withstand Mongolia's cold temperatures.

## Protected Areas

Mongolian religious beliefs hold that the land is sacred and must be protected. In the late twentieth century, this traditional belief system led to the creation of national parks and areas of Mongolia that would be preserved and protected. Bogd Khan is one of the world's oldest national parks. Its mountains have been protected since 1778.

Today, the nature reserve system in Mongolia has four levels. Strictly Protected Areas have the greatest ecological importance. These areas are considered significant to the world and will remain completely unspoiled and undeveloped. Natural Parks include wilderness areas that have historical, cultural, or environmental importance. Nature Reserves are dedicated to preserving a particular ecosystem or area, such as habitats, fossil beds, or rock formations. National or Historical Monuments protect natural and constructed monuments of historic, cultural, or touristic importance. Today, about 8 percent of Mongolia's lands are protected.

## Life Near Water

Mongolia's lakes and rivers support a rich variety of bird and plant life. Birds such as cormorants, great egrets, ducks, geese, terns, and gulls are common in many areas. Other birds such as swans, pelicans, cranes, ospreys, and fish eagles sometimes visit Mongolian waterways and lakes. Many low-lying marsh areas are filled with feather grass, couch grass, and wheatgrass.

## The Return of Mongolia's National Symbol

The story of Mongolia's national symbol, the *takhi*, is one of sadness, but it is also a story of hope. The takhi, a wild horse also known as Przewalski's horse, is the only genuine wild horse in the world. All other so-called wild horses are actually the descendants of domestic horses that escaped into the wild. The takhi has been part of the Mongolian landscape for millions of years. Along with other large grazing animals, it once lived throughout Europe and Asia. Some prehistoric cave paintings depict wild horses alongside other animals such as bison and elk.

As humans spread over the steppes and other lands in Europe, the takhi were forced into smaller and smaller areas. Eventually, they lived only in the Gobi Desert. By the turn of the twentieth century, hunters had killed almost all the wild horses. Habitat loss destroyed the herds as well. The takhi became extinct in the wild in 1969.

But unknown to most of the world, something had occurred that would lead to the survival of the takhi. Around 1900, traders and landowners had captured a group of takhi and sent them to Europe. Only fifty-three of the horses survived the trip. They were sent to zoos and private parks, where many died. But a few survived. Slowly, these last surviving takhi were bred with each other. Their numbers grew.

In the 1980s, several foundations, along with the Mongolian government, decided to reintroduce the takhi into the wild. By that time, almost one thousand captive takhi lived in Europe. They were all descended from just thirteen horses. A 50,000-acre (20,000-hectare) preserve was created in an unspoiled area of the Mongolian steppe. Today, this area is part of Khustai National Park. Between 1992 and 2000, eighty-five takhi were transported to their new home and released into the wild.

Today, there are about 150 wild horses in the preserve. The small herd that now gallops over the Mongolian steppe is a hopeful sign that one day the takhi will again be plentiful. The herd needs about five hundred horses to ensure that the species will survive in the wild, so the program still has a long way to go. But the symbol of Mongolia, the wild takhi, is now wild once again.

CHAPTER

FOUR

# A Rich
## and Violent
## History

M ONGOLIA STRETCHES OVER A VAST REGION, but modern Mongolia is only half the size Mongolia once was. During the height of the Mongolian empire, in the thirteenth and fourteenth centuries, Mongolia stretched from what is now Korea to Hungary. It included most of Asia except for the southeast and today's India. It was the largest empire of connecting land in the history of the world.

*Opposite:* **Genghis Khan's army attacks a fortress in northern China.**

**Thousands of years ago, people made pictures on rocks in the Gobi Desert.**

### The Beginning

Little is known about the earliest Mongols. Archaeologists have found evidence that people lived in the southern Gobi area between one hundred thousand and two hundred thousand years ago. Scientists have dug up primitive stone tools that were made by these people.

The earliest Mongolian written history dates back just eight hundred years. But Mongols recorded their history long before that, through oral storytelling and song. Other records also exist of their history. Because the Mongol empire was so vast, and because its leaders conquered so many other lands, the Mongols were written

about in many other languages. Many of these writers came from cultures that the Mongols controlled. So it is not surprising that they painted the Mongols as bloodthirsty warriors who were cruel to the people they conquered. The Chinese in particular described them as barbarians and wolves who were greedy for the wealth of China. For better or worse, the Mongols have one of the best-documented cultures in history.

The earliest written mention of a people living in Mongolia comes from ancient Chinese manuscripts dated to the fourth or fifth century B.C. They refer to "Turkik-speaking peoples" living in Mongolia during that time. The Chinese recorded many battles against this nomadic, warrior tribe they called the Xiongni. The Chinese and the Xiongni fought one another along their border for centuries. Eventually, the Xiongni were driven back for good.

The Chinese first used the term *Mongol* to describe nomadic warriors during China's Tang dynasty (A.D. 618–907). These nomads were probably people of the Uyghur culture, who had built several cities in the area.

## The Rise of Genghis Khan

By the end of the twelfth century, several different groups were scattered across Mongolia, including Mongols, Turks, Tanguts, and Tatars. There was no unified Mongol culture or society. But that would soon change.

In either 1162 or 1167 (historians can't agree on the date), a son was born to Yesugei, the powerful leader of the Borjigin Mongol clan. The boy was named Temujin. When

Temujin was about twelve years old, Yesugei was killed by one of his enemies, who poisoned him during a wedding ceremony. Temujin's clan rejected the boy as the new leader and left him and his family in the desert to die.

But Temujin didn't die. He survived, and by age twenty, he had become the leader of the Borjigin Mongol clan. For the next sixteen years, he fought to control the areas north of the Gobi Desert. Clans that had once been his enemies now allied with him. Year after year, Temujin conquered rival clans until he came to control the region between the Altai Mountains and Manchuria in China. In 1206, a special council of chieftains declared Temujin leader of all Mongolia, acknowledging him as their *khan*, or king. Temujin took the name *Genghis*, which means "Supreme" or "Great." The rest of the world would forever know him as Genghis Khan.

Genghis Khan was a great military leader. He united people from many different tribes into a single, powerful army.

## The Reign of the Great Khan

The next few years would see bloody warfare throughout Mongolia and the surrounding areas. Soon after he was declared khan, Genghis created his capital in Karakorum. (Its ruins are located in present-day Kharkhorin, about 200 miles [300 km] west of Ulaanbaatar.) Then he launched a huge offensive against China and Russia. First, he went south and defeated several Chinese groups, including the Tangut empire on the Yellow River and the Jin dynasty. In 1215, he sacked the great Jin city of Yanjing, which is now Beijing. His deadly army, with its expert bowmen, defeated every army set against it.

Genghis turned to Russia in 1219. Mongol troops thundered into the area of modern-day Kazakhstan and attacked. For the next six years, the Mongol army cut through Russia, conquering everything in its way. Finally, in 1225, Genghis returned to Mongolia. He was now the undisputed leader of the greatest kingdom in the world, which stretched millions of square miles across most of Asia.

Genghis Khan and his army fought their way across much of China in the 1210s. They took the Chinese capital in 1215.

## The Last Campaign

By now, Genghis was an old man. But he still wanted more power. In the winter of 1226, Genghis and his army headed south to China. Once again, his armies defeated several foes, including the Tanguts and a troop of Jin Chinese warriors. During this campaign, Genghis had the feeling that he would soon die. He turned around and headed back to Mongolia, but it was too late. He died before reaching home. His soldiers transported his body back to Mongolia, killing all those who crossed their path.

## The Mongol Empire After the Great Khan

Upon Genghis's death, control of his huge empire passed to his sons Tsagaadai and Ogedei, who continued to conquer more of China, Russia, and areas that are now Korea, Iran, and Syria. They also raided parts of what are now Poland and Lithuania. It seemed as if the Mongols would control the entire world.

Then, in 1241, the Mongol armies abruptly stopped. Without warning, they turned around and headed back to Mongolia. Tsagaadai and Ogedei had both died suddenly. Mongol law said that, after the death of a ruler, all the noble descendants of Genghis Khan had to return to Mongolia, no matter where

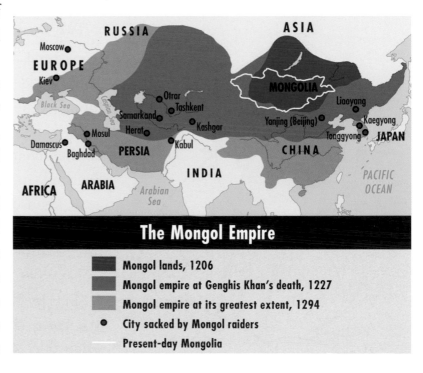

**The Mongol Empire**

■ Mongol lands, 1206
■ Mongol empire at Genghis Khan's death, 1227
■ Mongol empire at its greatest extent, 1294
● City sacked by Mongol raiders
— Present-day Mongolia

## The Sack of Baghdad

Hulegu Khan, a grandson of Genghis Khan, swept through the Middle East in the 1250s. In 1258, he and his huge army, which some say was the biggest Mongol army ever gathered, attacked Baghdad. After weeks of battles, the Mongol army entered the city and destroyed much of what they found there. The Grand Library of Baghdad, one of the greatest libraries of the time, was left in ruins. Mosques and palaces were burned to the ground. The Muslim leader was rolled in a carpet and trampled with horses. This was the Mongol way of killing royalty without spilling any blood. Historians estimate that several hundred thousand other Baghdad residents were also killed.

When Hulegu Khan and his army arrived in Baghdad, the city was one of the world's leading cultural centers. By the time Mongols left after sacking it, few people remained in the great city. It took Baghdad centuries to recover.

**The Mongols completed their conquest of China in 1279, during the reign of Khublai Khan.**

they were, to elect a new leader. The lands of Europe, Russia, and China were emptied of their Mongol conquerors. The Mongols would never again push so far into other territories.

### The Decline of the Mongol Empire

For a time, it seemed as if the Mongols would hold sway in the world forever. Mongke, a grandson of Genghis, was elected khan in 1251. During his reign, his brother Hulegu attacked and conquered Baghdad, in what is now Iraq. The next great khan, Khublai, continued the conquest of China and eventually destroyed this Song dynasty. Khublai Khan became emperor of China's Yuan dynasty.

But in 1260, the Mongols lost their first battle in almost one hundred years, when they were defeated by an Egyptian group known as the Mamelukes. Mongol invasions of Japan also failed. The Mongols had not experienced a failed conquest since Genghis Khan. Khublai Khan knew then that the Mongol empire had reached its limits. Instead of conquest, he focused on keeping his empire together. But it had already grown out of control. Khublai Khan was forced to fight many rival groups within the empire. He also had to fend off attacks from northern tribes. The Mongol empire had become too large for one person to rule.

Khublai Khan died in 1294. After his death, more than sixty thousand Mongols returned to Mongolia from the outlying areas, weakening the Mongol hold on the empire. Wars between rival clans broke out, destroying the unity that the Mongols once had. In 1368, the Mongols were

### Marco Polo Meets the Khan

When Marco Polo entered Khublai Khan's palace in 1275, he was about to meet one of the most powerful Mongols of all time. He described meeting the great ruler with his father and uncle:

*They knelt before him and made obeisance with the utmost humility. The Great Khan bade them rise and received them honorably and entertained them with good cheer. He asked many questions about their condition and how they fared after their departure. The brothers assured him that they had indeed fared well, since they found him well and flourishing. . . . When the Great Khan saw Marco, who was then a young stripling, he asked who he was. "Sir" said Messer Niccolò, "he is my son and your liege man." "He is heartily welcome," said the Khan. . . . Great indeed were the mirth and merry-making with which the Great Khan and all his Court welcomed the arrival of these emissaries. And they were well served and attended to in all their needs. They stayed at Court and had a place of honor above the other barons.*

A Mongolian official signs a treaty establishing diplomatic relations with the Soviet Union in 1921. The Soviet Union soon became a powerful influence in Mongolia.

expelled from Beijing by the Ming dynasty. Between 1400 and 1454, a bloody civil war pitted several Mongolian clans against one another and fragmented the culture even more. Slowly, the Mongols returned to a system of small, nomadic tribes.

Around 1644, a group called the Manchu founded the Qing dynasty in China. They eventually set out to conquer Mongolia. In 1691, the Mongols were defeated and came under the control of the Manchu, who ruled Mongolia for the next several hundred years.

## Revolution and Change

In 1911, the Qing dynasty of China finally crumbled. Since 1691, the Mongols had lived under the control of their Manchurian conquerors. With the end of the Qing dynasty, the Mongol leaders saw their chance. They declared independence. Russia became a close ally of the newly independent Mongolia.

Only a few years later, in 1917, the Russian Revolution shook Europe. The Russian people had forced their czar, or emperor, from power. Their revolution was led by communists, who believed that the government should own Russia's businesses and control its economy. Those opposing them were known as White Russians. Civil war soon shook the nation.

The Chinese took advantage of the chaos in Russia to invade Mongolia. Mongolia appealed to Russia for help in repelling the Chinese armies. Russian troops arrived and forced the Chinese army out of Mongolia. At first, Mongolian officials saw Russia as their friend and ally. But soon they realized that, in fact, Russia's aim was to control Mongolia itself.

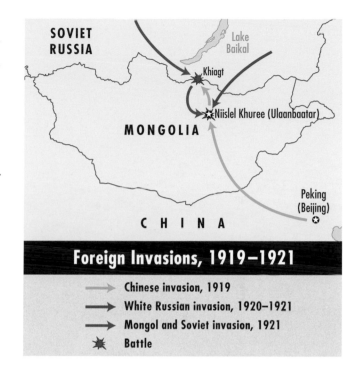

**Foreign Invasions, 1919–1921**

→ Chinese invasion, 1919
→ White Russian invasion, 1920–1921
→ Mongol and Soviet invasion, 1921
✹ Battle

In the 1920s, Russia joined with other countries in eastern Europe and central Asia to form a huge communist nation called the Soviet Union. It would become one of the most powerful nations on earth. In the late 1920s, the Soviet communist party began forcing Mongolia's government officials from power. They were replaced with communist politicians loyal to the Soviet Union. The communist politicians in Mongolia belonged to the Mongolian People's Revolutionary Party (MPRP). MPRP officials seized private property and took herds away from Mongolian nomads. Private business was outlawed. Religious leaders were executed by the thousands.

During the communist era, the Mongolian government limited the number of animals a person could own. Many herders tended both their own animals and some belonging to the government.

By the 1950s, the harshness of communist rule had subsided in Mongolia, and less-ruthless communist leaders controlled the country between the 1950s and 1970s. During that time, Mongolia enjoyed a measure of peace. Although most people worked on farms and in industries controlled by the government, some nomads with small herds survived. The outside world knew little of what was going in Mongolia during this time. The Soviet Union and Mongolia's communist leaders effectively locked the country away. Mongolia continued to be an unknown, mysterious place to the rest of the world.

## Democracy

In the late 1980s, massive political changes rumbled through the Soviet Union. During that time, Soviet leaders began a reform movement called *perestroika*. Under perestroika, private businesses were allowed. Noncommunist political parties were also legalized, and a parliament, or legislature, was created.

The Mongolian people sensed what was coming. Pro-democracy demonstrations were held in the capital city of Ulaanbaatar. In 1990, the communist leaders in the Mongolian government resigned. The Mongolian Constitution was soon changed to allow for democratic elections. Mongolia had transformed from a nation controlled by a communist party to a democratic country, without a shot being fired.

Since the fall of communism in Mongolia, the nation has slowly opened to the rest of the world. Curious tourists, mostly hearty types, brave the harsh climate and vast expanses of land to see this mysterious place. What they find today is a country in transition. The nomadic lifestyle of livestock owners—the Mongols way of life for centuries—is declining. Urban life is on the rise. Meanwhile, the democratic government continues to struggle to lead a country filled with people who remember the reliable roads and stable economy under the communist regime.

A crowd gathers for a demonstration in the capital in 1990. The protesters were demanding democratic changes in Mongolia.

CHAPTER

FIVE

# A Government in Transition

50

THROUGHOUT MOST OF THE TWENTIETH CENTURY, Mongolia was a communist nation. As the twenty-first century began, Mongolians confronted the challenge of a new government system based on democracy and freedom.

*Opposite:* **Ulaanbaatar is a startling mix of the old and the new.**

### Mongolia Before 1992

Prior to 1992, Mongolians lived under a government modeled after the Soviet Union's communist system. Under this form of government, only one political party, the Mongolian People's Revolutionary Party (MPRP), was allowed to exist. People were not permitted to own property or businesses, and most Mongolians

**A Soviet soldier stands guard in Ulaanbaatar. Soviet troops were stationed in Mongolia from 1966 until 1992.**

lived and worked on farms or in industries controlled by the government. For the most part, Mongolia enjoyed a measure of peace and prosperity under communist rule.

The rise of perestroika in the Soviet Union brought changes to the Mongolian government system. The first Mongolian pro-democracy demonstrations occurred in Ulaanbaatar in 1989, when the wave of perestroika

began to wash over other communist countries. Soon, a pro-democracy movement swept through Mongolia. One group, the Mongolian Democratic Union, became powerful in this push for democracy. Less than a year later, the communist leadership of the MPRP resigned their government positions.

Later that year, the Mongolian Constitution was changed to create a new government that included a legislature called the People's Great Khural. It also established the office of president. Under the old system, the communist party (MPRP) was the only party allowed. The new constitution legalized other political parties. In July 1990, Mongolia held its first multiparty election, in which the members of the People's Great Khural were chosen.

In November 1991, the People's Great Khural created an entirely new constitution for the nation. It took effect in

## Mongolia's Flag

The flag of Mongolia was adopted in 1992. It has three equal vertical stripes of color, which are red, blue, and red. Blue is the country's national color. Red, which once stood for communism, now stands for progress. Centered in the middle of the left red band, in yellow, is the national emblem. This emblem is a symbol called the *soyombo*. It represents fire, the sun, the moon, the earth, and water. In the center of the soyombo is a yin and yang symbol. This round design with two parts that wrap around each other represents the idea that everything in life is connected and balanced.

February 1992. The new constitution created many new laws and guidelines for the young government. It said that the president would be elected by the people, rather than by the legislature. It guaranteed a number of rights and freedoms, such as the rights to free speech and religious freedom. It also restructured the legislative branch of government, creating a parliament called the State Great Khural.

Voter turnout has been high in the years since Mongolia began having free elections. In 2005, 75 percent of eligible voter cast ballots in the presidential election.

## Mongolian National Anthem

The "National Anthem of Mongolia" was first adopted in 1951. The music is by Bilegiyn Damdinsuren and Luvsanyamts Muryorj, and the words are by Tsendiyn Damdinsuren.

**Mongolian lyrics**

*Dar khan manai khuvsgalt ulas*
*Dalaar mongolyn ariun golomtoo*
*Daisny khold khezeech orokhgui*
*Dandaa enkhzhizh uurd monkhzhene.*

*CHORUS:*
*Khamag delkhiin shudarga ulastai*
*Khamtran negdsen egneeg bekhzhuulzhee*
*Khatan zorig bukhii chadlaaraa*
*Khairtai mongol ornoo manduuliaa.*

*Zorigt mongolyin zoltoi arduud*
*Zovlong tonilgozh zhargalyg edlev*
*Zhargalyn tulkhuur khogzhliin tulguur*
*Zhavkhlant manai oron mandtugai.*

*CHORUS*

**English translation**

*Our sacred revolutionary country*
*Is the ancestral hearth of all Mongols,*
*No enemy will defeat us,*
*And we will prosper for eternity.*

*CHORUS:*
*Our country will strengthen relations*
*With all righteous countries of the world.*
*And let us develop our beloved Mongolia*
*With all our will and might.*

*The glorious people of the brave Mongolia*
*Have defeated all sufferings, and gained happiness,*
*The key to delight, and the path to progress —*
*Majestic Mongolia — our country, live forever!*

*CHORUS*

## The Executive Branch

In Mongolia's executive branch, political power is divided between two people: the president and the prime minister. The president is elected by popular vote to a four-year term, with a limit of two terms. He or she must be a native citizen of Mongolia and be at least forty-five years old. The president must have lived in Mongolia for five years before the election.

The president serves as chief of state, commander in chief of the armed forces, and head of the National Security Council. The constitution gives the president the power to nominate a prime minister, create legislation, veto (reject) all or part of any legislation, and issue decrees. The president can also call for the disbanding of the government. Mongolia has no vice president. If the president can no longer fulfill his or her duties as leader, the chairman of the State Great Khural is given the president's power until a new president is elected.

The prime minister serves a four-year term. It is the prime minister's job to choose a cabinet, which is then approved by the State Great Khural.

Miyeegombiin Enkhbold became prime minister in 2006. He is the former mayor of Ulaanbaatar.

Mongolia has a single-house parliament, the State Great Khural. It has seventy-six members who are elected by popular vote to four-year terms. The members elect a chairman and a vice chairman, each of whom serves for four years.

The State Great Khural meets in the Government House. It is located in Sükhbaatar Square in the heart of Ulaanbaatar.

The members of the State Great Khural have many responsibilities, including enacting laws, creating foreign and domestic policy, and approving international agreements. They can also declare a state of emergency if needed. The State Great Khural can override a presidential veto with a two-thirds majority vote.

Sanjaasurengin Oyan was one of five female members of parliament in 2005. She is the head of the Citizen's Will Party.

## The Judicial Branch

Mongolia's system of government includes a Constitutional Court, which interprets the country's constitution. The Constitutional Court consists of nine justices who are appointed to six-year terms. This group makes sure that the rules set forth in the constitution are followed.

The General Council of Courts (GCC) chooses all judges who serve in Mongolia's lower courts. The GCC also nominates judges to the Supreme Court, Mongolia's highest court. Supreme Court judges are confirmed by the State Great Khural and the

### GOVERNMENT OF MONGOLIA

**Executive Branch**

PRESIDENT

PRIME MINISTER

**Legislative Branch**

STATE GREAT KHURAL
(76 MEMBERS)

**Judicial Branch**

CONSTITUTIONAL COURT      SUPREME COURT

LOWER COURTS

Many Mongolians took to the streets of Ulaanbaatar for a protest in 2006. They called for an end to government corruption and a change in government leadership.

president. The Supreme Court has the power to review lower court decisions and provide official interpretations of all laws except the constitution.

## The Unsteady Hold of Democracy

Democracy has not come easily to Mongolia. Since 1992, the country has had several major upheavals in its government. Communists won most of the first elections. The MPRP assured the Mongolian people that the democratic changes they had promised would be fulfilled. In 1996, the MPRP lost the elections to the Democratic Coalition Party. It was the first time in seventy-five years that the MPRP was not in control of the Mongolian government. But the Democratic Coalition government was inexperienced and made many mistakes. Between 1996 and 2000, Mongolia went through four prime ministers. Many government officials were accused of corruption.

In 2000, MPRP member Nambariin Enkhbayar was chosen as prime minister. In 2004, the Mongolian people threw out the MPRP once again and voted for Democratic Coalition candidates. Forty-one-year-old Tsakhiagiin Elbegdorj, a former journalist, became prime minister.

In January 2006, another upheaval rocked the Mongolian government. Thirty-nine members of parliament, most of them MPRP members, overthrew Elbegdorj and the government. They then elected Miyeegombiin Enkhbold as prime minister, and Enkhbayar returned as president.

Mongolia was in an uproar. Citizens around the country staged protests against the MPRP's overthrow of the government. Accusations flew on all sides. The MPRP accused Elbegdorj's government of corruption. Others accused the MPRP of being afraid that its own corruption would have been revealed by Elbegdorj's government.

Through all the changes, Mongolia has been slowly working its way toward political stability. It may be a long road, for democracy is still young in Mongolia.

President Nabariin Enkhbayer (right) shakes hands with Miyeegombiin Enkhbold in 2006 after Enkhbold was chosen to be prime minister.

## Ulaanbaatar: Did You Know This?

Ulaanbaatar, the capital of Mongolia, lies in a valley in the east-central part of the country. The main road through this valley is called Enkh Taivnii Orgon Choloo, which translates to "Peace Avenue." Beautiful mountains surround the city.

Home to 850,000 people, Ulaanbaatar is by far the largest and most cosmopolitan city in Mongolia. Many visitors to Ulaanbaatar expect the city to be a throwback to the days of the Mongol empire, with people sipping drinks in dark cafés and exotic goods for sale. What they find instead is a growing city filled with a mix of gray concrete-box buildings and bright, modern shops and restaurants. The streets are filled with businesspeople, backpacking tourists, Buddhist monks, and nomads from the steppes.

Through its history, Ulaanbaatar has been known by many names. When it was founded in 1639 as a monastery town, it was called Orgoo. Later, it was called the City of Felt, because it consisted mainly of felt gers, tents that could be moved from place to place. Still later, the city was known as Ikh Khuree, or "the Great Camp." The city became the capital of Mongolia in 1911, when the country gained its independence from the Manchu. At that time, it was renamed again, this time to Niislel Khuree, which means "Capital Camp." In 1924, after Russia gained great influence

in Mongolia, the city got its current name, Ulaanbaatar, which means "Red Hero," in honor of Sükhbaatar, a local communist hero. When communism ended in 1990, Mongolians chose to keep the name.

For most of its history, Ulaanbaatar's economy has been based on trade and industry. It lies at the junction of several old caravan roads between Russia and China. In the 1950s, a major railroad was built through the area. Called the Trans-Siberian Railway, it links Russia with China. Today, the city has factories that produce goods such as woolen textiles, leather, footwear, soap, paper, glassware, cement, and processed foods.

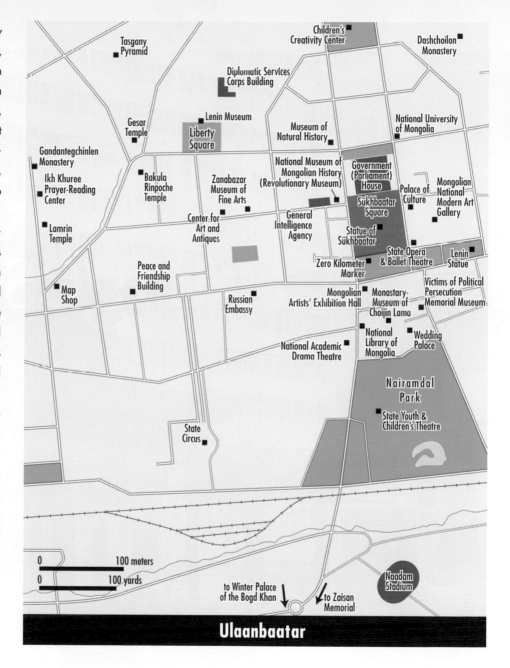

Ulaanbaatar

# Economic
# Changes

Mongolia's economy has weathered great change in recent history. In the last twenty years, it has gone from a communist economy to a free-market economy. No longer are prices fixed and jobs assured. The change has been difficult for many people. In many ways, Mongolia is still trying to find its way economically, both at home and in the global market.

*Opposite:* **Many modern office buildings have been constructed in Ulaanbaatar in recent years.**

**Farmers stand near bales of hay on the Mongolian steppe.**

## From Agriculture to Industry

Before communism took hold of Mongolia in the 1920s, the country's economy was based on herding. Most Mongolians lived as nomads with their herds of sheep and cattle. They raised or traded for whatever they needed. A few industries provided other goods, but manufacturing was a small part of the economy.

Communism transformed the Mongolian economy. With the Soviet Union's help, Mongolia's communist government began building huge factories and creating large collective farms and herds. The government helped farms by setting

A horse pulls a cart loaded down with hay in 1961. During Mongolia's communist years, the government turned some steppe into agricultural land.

prices for crops and animals. Industries such as coal and gold mining grew under communist control. By the 1960s, Mongolia's economy had become completely dependent on government-controlled industries and collective agriculture.

In the 1980s, the Mongolian government began large-scale mining, especially for gold and copper. This created a huge need for more electricity to run the mining operations, so power plants were built. The Soviet Union helped pay for many of these changes. At the same time, the government fixed prices, even though manufacturing costs were increasing. Again the Soviets gave Mongolia whatever aid it needed to keep the factories and industries running.

A huge copper mine opened near Erdenet in 1960. It is the fifth-largest copper mine in the world.

After communism ended in Mongolia, many state-run factories fell into ruins. Today, it is estimated that as many as 20 percent of adult Mongolians cannot find jobs.

## Economic Collapse

When change swept through the Soviet Union in the late 1980s, Mongolia's economy was greatly affected. Mongolia had been dependent on the Soviet Union for almost all of its trade, for fuel, for medicine, and for the maintenance of power plants and factories. Suddenly, the Soviet Union stopped all financial aid and canceled projects. The aid that had propped up Mongolian industry and agriculture vanished. Power plants and factories shut down. Road building and transportation projects stopped.

The country was faced with 325 percent inflation, which means an item that originally cost $1 would cost $325 a year later. There were shortages of every kind. This led to rationing—limiting how much of certain items people could buy. Rationing had not happened in Mongolia since the 1940s, during World War II. At the same time, manufacturing was almost wiped out. Certain types of farming collapsed. The Mongolian currency dropped in value.

The new democratic government tried to solve these problems by making several reforms. It gradually phased out the system of fixing prices. It opened up businesses to private ownership. A new banking system was created. The government started trading with other countries to replace its reliance on Soviet trade. The government also passed laws that encouraged competition.

The Mongolian economy went into a tailspin in the 1990s. Basic good were rationed, and people had to stand in line to buy milk.

## The Modern Economy

Slowly, the Mongolian economy began to recover. By the mid-1990s, annual inflation had fallen to 66 percent, and by 2000 it was at a manageable 8.1 percent. The government began a program of privatization. Under privatization, individuals could own land, herds, and businesses. Thousands of Mongolians returned to the nomadic and farming ways of life. Agriculture grew. Although industry never recovered from the collapse, mining rose to become a large part of the Mongolian economy. Trade has also grown.

More than 40 percent of Mongolians make their living herding livestock. An estimated 3.5 million head of cattle graze on the nation's vast grasslands.

## Mongolian Money

The unit of currency in Mongolia is the togrog, also known as the tugrik. About 1,120 togrogs equal one U.S. dollar. The word *togrog* means "round." Togrogs come in bills of 5, 10, 20, 50, 100, 500, 1,000, 5,000 and 10,000 togrogs.

Togrogs became the official currency in Mongolia in 1925. Before that, Mongolians used foreign money or traded such items as gold rubles from Russia, bricks of tea, or silver ingots. During the rule of Genghis Khan, coins called *sukh,* made of gold or silver, were used as money. During Manchu rule, various Chinese currencies were used. But traders preferred Russian gold, British money, and trade goods such as tea, milk, wool, silk, and furs.

The current designs on the togrog notes were adopted in 1992. The small bills feature a portrait of Damdin Sükhbaatar, a military leader, on the front. Bills of 500 togrogs and more depict Genghis Khan on the front. The back of the 500 togrog note shows animals pulling a ger.

Though Mongolia has made great economic strides, its success has been mixed. In the late 1990s and early 2000s, a combination of droughts and severe winters, called *dzuds*, destroyed much of the herding and agricultural economy. Many power plants that supplied electricity under communist rule have not been revived or replaced, so areas that once enjoyed a healthy industrial economy are now depressed. Some industries are plagued by corruption and mismanagement. But as each problem is solved, the Mongolian economy will continue to strengthen.

More than three million horses range across Mongolia. Mongolian horses are short, stocky, and sturdy.

## Agriculture

Agriculture has always been the backbone of the Mongolian economy. Today, it continues to play a strong role in the economic health of the country. Most of Mongolian agriculture is based on livestock. Almost half the labor force in Mongolia works with livestock. Today, more than 97 percent of livestock herds are privately owned. About 256,000 Mongolian families own their own herds. The five major livestock animals in Mongolia are horses, cattle,

### What Mongolia Grows, Makes, and Mines

**Agriculture (2002)**

| | |
|---|---|
| Livestock | 23,900,000 head |
| Wheat | 110,000 metric tons |
| Potatoes | 45,000 metric tons |

**Manufacturing**

| | |
|---|---|
| Cement (2002) | 148,000 metric tons |
| Lime (2002) | 41,000 metric tons |
| Carpets (2000) | 705,000 square meters |

**Mining**

| | |
|---|---|
| Coal (2000) | 833,000 metric tons |
| Copper (2001) | 135,503 metric tons |
| Gold (2001) | 13,675 kilograms |

camels, sheep, and goats. In 2002, there were 23.9 million head of livestock in Mongolia.

Weather plays a big role in agriculture. Any severe weather can affect the overall economy. The droughts and severe winters that ended in the early 2000s killed hundreds of thousands of animals. Many nomadic families lost their entire herds. The long-term impact of this devastating weather is still not fully known.

Crops also play an important role in the Mongolian economy. More than 542,500 acres (220,000 hectares) are planted with crops such as cereals, potatoes, vegetables, and grains grown as livestock feed. In 2002, Mongolians grew 121,000 tons (110,000 metric tons) of wheat, 49,000 tons (45,000 metric tons) of potatoes, and 38,000 tons (35,000 metric tons) of vegetables.

**Mongolia's Hairy Treasure**

Mongolia's richest resource is an unlikely one: the hair of animals such as sheep, goats, camels, yaks, and horses. Fine woolen products come from sheep. Goats produce the rich, soft hair that is known as cashmere. Each year, Mongolia produces up to 3,000 tons (2,700 metric tons) of cashmere wool, which is then used to make products such as blankets and clothing. Camel hair is made into blankets and carpets. Yak hair becomes yarn. And the manes and tails of horses are used to make rope.

Industry was hit the hardest after the end of communism in 1990. Most industries and factories in Mongolia had been controlled by the government. The goods they manufactured were exported to the Soviet Union and other communist countries. When communism ended, the Mongolian industrial economy collapsed. Although there has been some recovery, industry is not as significant a part of the economy as it once was.

The biggest problem for industry is that there is no money to buy raw materials from other countries. As a result, the industries that have developed in Mongolia rely on raw materials that can be grown or found within the country. Industries that make wool, leather, textiles, metals, and food products are on the rise. Today, Mongolia exports products such as cashmere, knitwear, blankets, and carpets to more than forty countries around the world.

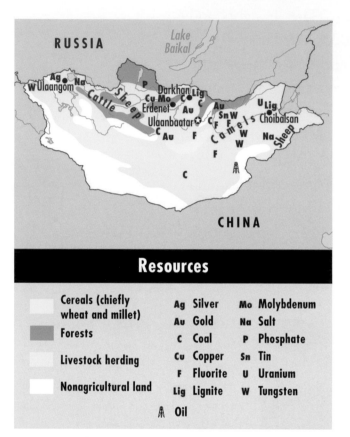

## Resources

| | | | |
|---|---|---|---|
| Cereals (chiefly wheat and millet) | Ag | Silver | Mo Molybdenum |
| Forests | Au | Gold | Na Salt |
| | C | Coal | P Phosphate |
| Livestock herding | Cu | Copper | Sn Tin |
| | F | Fluorite | U Uranium |
| Nonagricultural land | Lig | Lignite | W Tungsten |
| | Oil | | |

Food processing is also increasing in Mongolia. Many small- and medium-sized factories around the country make milk products, serve as flour mills, and process meat. Much of this food is exported to China and Russia.

## Mining

Mongolia is rich in mineral resources, and mining has become a vital part of the economy. Between 15 and 16 percent of all Mongolian land is dedicated to mining operations. It is a healthy part of the economy, enjoying 8 percent growth each year. More than four hundred different minerals and other natural resources have been found in Mongolia. These include coal, copper, fluorite, iron ore, gold, silver, zinc, and lead. Mongolia also has deposits of stone, sand, gravel, limestone, and marble.

Coal was the first resource to be mined on a large scale in Mongolia. The communist government built the country's first coal mine in the town of Nalaikh, near Ulaanbaatar, in the 1930s. Other mines at Erdenet, Darkhan, Choir, and Mardai extracted coal, copper, iron ore, and uranium. Many mines shut down in the 1990s after the Soviet Union collapsed.

Most coal mined in Mongolia stays in the country and is used to make electricity. Some is also exported to Russia.

In recent years, the government has increased production of coal, most of which is used in Mongolia. It is estimated that Mongolia might have up to 138 billion tons (125 billion metric tons) of coal reserves. But the country currently does not have the roads or railways to transport it. For instance, a huge coal deposit has been found in the Gobi, but it is located more than 250 miles (400 km) from the nearest railway. With no money to build roads, many of Mongolia's rich coal deposits remain untouched for the time being.

The government also hopes to increase the country's oil output. Mongolia began exporting oil in 1997 on a small scale. Since the fall of communism, the government has allowed companies from the United States, China, and Australia to explore for oil around the country.

## Tourism

Until 1990, tourism was virtually unheard of in Mongolia. A state tourism company, Juulchin, had been created in 1954, but tourism was tightly controlled by the communist government. When the Soviet Union collapsed in 1991, Mongolia began opening its borders to visitors from around the world. In 1993, only about 8,000 foreign tourists came to Mongolia. By 2005, that number had increased to 338,000. Today, tourism is an important part of the Mongolian economy. It accounts for about 10 percent of the total value of goods and services produced in Mongolia.

Tourists come to Mongolia to experience the breathtaking mountains, the endless steppes, and the Gobi Desert. Some visitors come to hunt exotic animals such as ibex. One of the unique experiences of a trip to Mongolia is visiting with the nomads of the steppes and staying in a traditional ger. Today, tourism continues to grow throughout Mongolia, as the country is seen as one of the last unspoiled places on earth.

Many visitors to Mongolia try riding horses across the steppe. It is an ideal way to see the sweeping landscape.

# Being Mongolian

Most Mongolian nomads live in round huts, but the Tsaatan people use cone-shaped tents.

THE LAND AND THE NOMADIC LIFESTYLE HAVE SHAPED almost every aspect of the lives of Mongolia's people. For centuries, Mongolians moved with their herds, going wherever the land and the weather took them. This gave them a deep love for the land and for freedom. Modern Mongolia has also been affected by the long years of communism and by the swift changes that have happened recently. These influences have combined to give Mongolians a unique outlook on life that combines ancient traditions with new ideas.

*Opposite:* **Mongolians maintain a strong connection to the land.**

The nomadic Tsaatan people live in northern Mongolia. They raise reindeer, which they use for transportation, milk, and meat.

The nomadic people of Mongolia have learned how to live in harmony with their surroundings. They have adapted to the country's extreme environments and weather. The key to their survival is their mobility. They can move from areas that are not suited for grazing to places that are better for themselves and their livestock.

Rural nomads and people who live in the cities tend to have a big difference in attitudes. Mongolians in the cities tend to act more "Western" and enjoy all the advantages that a city has to offer. The rural nomads live with few possessions and revere the natural world. Most of the country's political and economic changes have not affected the nomads the way they have people in the city. Nomads take the changes in stride and keep moving. Though the nomads have few possessions, they have a rich culture and traditions that are part of the Mongolian spirit.

**The Population of Mongolia's Major Cities**

| | |
|---|---|
| Ulaanbaatar | 850,000 |
| Erdenet | 68,310 |
| Darkhan | 65,791 |
| Choibalsan | 41,000 |

A nomadic family erects a ger. It takes about an hour to put one up.

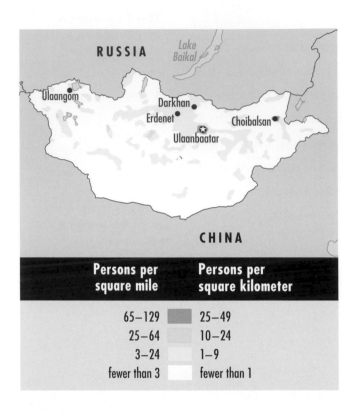

| Persons per square mile | Persons per square kilometer |
|---|---|
| 65–129 | 25–49 |
| 25–64 | 10–24 |
| 3–24 | 1–9 |
| fewer than 3 | fewer than 1 |

Cold weather wiped out whole herds of livestock in the winter of 1999–2000. About three million animals died.

When communism collapsed in 1990, many Mongolians lost their jobs in factories and other businesses that had received financial aid from the Soviet Union. Many of these people bought livestock and returned to the steppes, with the hope that they could make a living as herders. Some of them made it. But many realized they were unsuited to the harsh conditions and poverty of nomadic life. Also, when severe weather destroyed thousands of herds in the early 2000s, some people were forced to return to the cities to find work.

## Who Lives in Mongolia?

| | |
|---|---|
| Mongolians | 98% |
| Chinese | 1% |
| Russians | 1% |

In 1921, only 60,000 people lived in Ulaanbaatar. Today, it has a population of about 850,000.

Since 2001, Mongolia's population has gradually shifted back to urban areas. The capital, Ulaanbaatar, is the fastest-growing city in Mongolia. It has grown by roughly thirty thousand people each year since 1999.

Today, about half the people in Mongolia live in urban areas. Around one-quarter live as nomads year-round. The rest of the people of Mongolia are seminomadic—they spend most of their time with their herds on the steppes, only returning to permanent villages during the winter.

Gers are always set up with their doors facing south. This helps keep out the cold, brutal wind that whips down from the north.

| Population of Mongol Ethnic Groups | |
| --- | --- |
| Khalkh | 2,300,000 |
| Durvud | 55,000 |
| Buryat | 45,000 |
| Bayad | 40,000 |
| Zakhchin | 24,700 |
| Dariganga | 32,300 |
| Uriankhai | 21,000 |
| Darkhad | 15,000 |
| Uuld | 11,400 |
| Torguud | 10,500 |
| Khoton | 6,000 |
| Myangad | 5,000 |
| Barga | 1,560 |
| Tsaatan | 200 |
| Uzemchin | 200 |

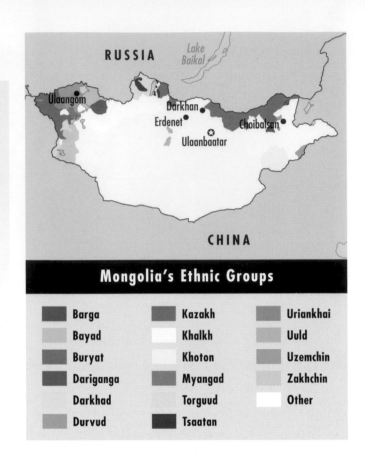

Mongolia's Ethnic Groups

Barga
Bayad
Buryat
Dariganga
Darkhad
Durvud
Kazakh
Khalkh
Khoton
Myangad
Torguud
Tsaatan
Uriankhai
Uuld
Uzemchin
Zakhchin
Other

## Ethnic Groups

The vast majority of people in Mongolia are ethnic Mongols. Though they may be descended from different tribes, or clans, there are few real ethnic differences. They all consider themselves Mongolian. The Khalkh Mongols form the largest of these ethnic groups, making up about 86 percent of the population. Small numbers of Russians and Chinese also live in Mongolia.

## The Mongolian Language

Mongolian is the official language of Mongolia. It has several dialects, or versions. The most common is Khalkha Mongolian. Traditionally, Mongolian was written using the Uyghur alpha-

## Speak Like a Mongolian

| Cyrillic letter | Latin letter | Pronounced | Cyrillic letter | Latin letter | Pronounced |
|---|---|---|---|---|---|
| а | a | as the *u* in cut | У | ü | as the *oo* in boo |
| Г | г | as the *g* in gum | Ц | ts | as in bats |
| Ё | yo | as in yonder | Щ | shch | as the *shch* in "wash child" |
| И | i | as in bin | | | |
| Л | l | as in lamb | Ь | | a symbol that makes the letter before it soft |
| О | o | as in stop | | | |
| Р | r | as in rust | Я | ya | as in yarn |
| У | u | as in glue | В | v | as in violin |
| Х | kh | as the *ch* in Scottish loch | Е | ye | as in yet |
| Ш | sh | as in ship | | yö | as the *yea* in yearn |
| Ы | y | as the *i* in fill | З | z | as the *ds* in muds |
| Ю | yu | as the *yo* in yodel | К | k | as in kitten |
| | yü | like the word you | Н | n | as in net |
| Б | b | as in boat | П | p | as in pin |
| Д | d | as in door | Т | t | as in toy |
| Ж | j | as in jam | Ф | f | as in fine |
| Й | i | as in rim | Ч | ch | as in charm |
| М | m | as in mark | Ъ | | a symbol that makes the letter before it hard |
| Ө | ö | as the *u* in fur | | | |
| С | s | as in soft | Э | e | as in lend |

bet, which was first used by the Uyghur people who lived in what is now western China. Since the 1930s, after the Soviet Union came to dominate the country, Mongolian has been written using a version of the Cyrillic alphabet. This is the alphabet of the Russian language.

## Common Mongolian Words and Phrases

| | |
|---|---|
| *Sain baina uu* | Hello |
| *Bayartai* | Good-bye |
| *Tiim* | Yes |
| *Ügüi* | No |
| *Bayarlaa* | Thanks |
| *Uuchlaarai* | Excuse me |
| *Tany neriig khen ge-deg ve* | What is your name? |
| *Minii neriig* | My name is . . . |
| *Sonin salkhan yu baina?* | What's new? |
| *To kheden nastai ve?* | How old are you? |
| *Bid airag uukh gesen yum.* | We'd like to drink some airag. |

Mongolian can be difficult for Westerners to learn. Both its sound and its grammar are very different from what they are used to.

### A Tradition of Hospitality

Whether they live in a city or far out on the steppes, Mongolians are known for their welcoming ways with outsiders. Hospitality to everyone is one of the most important aspects of life in Mongolia.

The harshness of the land has created a kinship among the people who live on the steppes. In the vast, empty land, people have to rely on one another for supplies, friendship, and news. In fact, hospitality is a big part of their survival. Every person is a potential doctor, mechanic, trader, or friend.

It is the duty of every person to welcome any visitor into their ger, a round hut made of a wood frame covered with felt. Usually Mongolians will offer the guest hot tea and simple foods such as cheese and candy. Once the visitor is refreshed, the family may ask a few questions. Guests are obligated to accept the food and drink that is offered.

Travelers to Mongolia marvel at the fact that it is possible to cross the country without spending any money on food or lodging. The Mongolian people consider it rude or shameful to ask for money. Most guests return the kindness by offering the family small gifts or candy for the children.

*Opposite:* **In Mongolia, guests are always welcomed warmly and offered food and drink. These visitors are sampling** *airag,* **a drink make from horse's milk.**

## Hospitality Customs

The Mongolian people have several customs that they observe every time they visit another ger. An approaching visitor calls out "*Nokhoi khorioroi,*" which means "Catch the dog." Someone from the family comes out and invites him or her inside. Any weapons the visitor has must be left at the door. The visitor doesn't knock on the door. Instead, he clears his throat to signal that he is about to enter the ger. Visitors always cross the threshold of the ger with their right foot first. Usually a younger person greets an older person first, saying "*Ta sain baina uu?*" This means "How are you?" or "How do you do?"

Mongolians do not normally shake hands. Instead, they greet visitors by stretching their arms to one another. Once these customs have been completed, the visitor is seated in the ger and offered food and drink.

## Close Quarters

A Mongolian ger is the center of the lives of the people who live there. These sturdy huts can withstand the high winds and biting temperatures of the steppes. Gers have helped to shape Mongolian family life. Everyone lives together in a one-room ger. Cooperation and patience are a necessary part of life.

Mongolian hospitality is not just found on the steppes. It is common for people in the city to show up at a friend's house without warning. The friend will treat the visitor just as a nomad would welcome a stranger into a ger. This is not just a nice tradition—it is a deep and lasting part of Mongolian culture.

In most of Mongolia, people are few and far between. New faces are always welcome.

# Spiritual Life

R ELIGION AND SPIRITUAL BELIEFS IN MONGOLIA ARE A mix of ancient traditions and modern customs. Buddhism was the dominant religion in Mongolia for centuries. But when communism took hold of Mongolia in the early twentieth century, almost all aspects of the rich Buddhist culture and faith were destroyed. Only since 1990 have the Mongolian people been free to rediscover the religious beliefs and practices from their past. Today, most Mongolians again practice Buddhism.

*Opposite:* **The Erdene Zuu monastery dates back to 1585.**

**Many Buddhist temples have prayer wheels. Spinning a wheel is like saying the blessing written on the wheel.**

## Buddhism

Buddhism is a religious belief system based on the teachings of Siddhartha Gautama, also known as Buddha. Buddhism rejects the idea that humans have an immortal soul and that there is a supreme god. Instead, Buddhism teaches that people should try to become free from greed, anger, and hatred by following the path to enlightenment.

Buddhism began in India and spread to Mongolia in the thirteenth century, during the time of Khublai Khan. By the fifteen century, Buddhism was the major religion of the Mongolian people.

**Before the communist era, the leader of Tibetan Buddhism in Mongolia was the Bogd Khan. The palace of the Bogd Khan is now a museum.**

The Erdene Zuu monastery was built on the site of the Karakorum, Genghis Khan's capital city.

## A Bloody Religious Past

For more than seven hundred years, Mongolia was a deeply Buddhist country. The people followed Buddhist beliefs as part of their daily lives. Buddhist monasteries were centers of education and medicine. Buddhist leaders also served as local officials in many places. Buddhism was part of the fabric of Mongolian culture and life.

When the communists took control of Mongolia in the 1920s, about three thousand Buddhist monasteries and temples were scattered throughout the country. More than eighty-seven thousand monks, or religious leaders, lived in these monasteries, and monks made up about half of the male population. More than eighteen thousand children attended school in Buddhist monasteries, which owned 21 percent of all livestock.

At first, the communist government attacked Buddhism by making laws that banned certain people from becoming monks. The new government opened new public schools to provide children with an education that was not religious, and soon the monasteries were no longer allowed to provide education. Communist writers began accusing religious leaders of many crimes. The communists encouraged people to destroy Buddhist temples and sacred objects. Any monks who were of military age were fined for not being in the army.

By the early 1930s, the communists were arresting and executing monks throughout the country. In 1934, Soviet leader Joseph Stalin became focused on destroying Mongolia's monasteries. He placed loyal Communist Party officials in the Mongolian government and instructed them to carry out his demands. The final push to eliminate the religion from Mongolia had begun.

Tens of thousands of monks were rounded up and executed. Others were either imprisoned or forced to leave religious life. All monasteries were closed, and most of them were destroyed. A few were turned into museums. The livestock herds that were owned by the monasteries were given to collective farms. The monasteries' wealth, including precious metals, was stolen and used by the government.

Almost every Buddhist temple and monastery in Mongolia was destroyed in the 1930s.

During the years of communist rule, it was illegal to practice Buddhism or any other religion in Mongolia. But Buddhism continued to be practiced in secret by many Mongolians. Nomads in remote areas followed Buddhist beliefs. They kept the rituals and holidays of the religion safe and passed this knowledge down to their children.

## The First Spiritual Leader of Mongolia

In the late 1630s, the Buddhists of Tibet and Mongolia were searching for a new spiritual leader. All of the signs pointed to a three-year-old named Zanabazar, a descendant of Genghis Khan. He became the first spiritual head of Buddhism in Mongolia.

When Zanabazar was only eight years old, he was recognized as being a "living Buddha" and taken to the monastery of Da Khuree. In 1647, he founded the Shankh monastery.

Zanabazar encouraged the arts, theology, language, astronomy, and medicine. His most lasting achievement is the creation of the Soyombo Mongolian script in 1686. Today, Soyombo is used mainly for sacred and ornamental Buddhist documents.

After the end of communism in Mongolia in the early 1990s, people were once again free to follow the Buddhist faith. But there were no monasteries left to worship in. Slowly, the people of Mongolia are reviving their ancient practices and celebrations. The Buddhist rituals, which were passed down through families, are again being conducted in public. New monasteries have opened, and they have, in turn, opened schools. Government projects to rebuild or restore old temples are in the works.

Since communism ended in Mongolia, many people have returned to the practice of Buddhism. More than three thousand Buddhist monks now live in the country.

## Gandan Khiid, Ulaanbaatar's Great Monastery

One of the few surviving Buddhist monasteries in Mongolia is Gandantegchilen (or Gandan) Khiid. Its name means "the Great Palace of Complete Joy." It is the largest monastery in the country and one of the main tourist sites in Ulaanbaatar.

Construction of the monastery began in 1838. It was a major seat of learning and religion in Mongolia until the communist government tried to destroy Buddhism in the 1930s. As at all monasteries in Mongolia, Gandan's monks were executed and its wealth confiscated. But the communists did not destroy the temple itself. In fact, the temple survived in part because of a U.S. government leader.

In 1944, the U.S. vice president, Henry Wallace, visited Mongolia and asked to see a Buddhist temple. The prime minister, Khorloin Choibalsan, needed to find a monastery that had not been destroyed. He hurriedly reopened Gandan, hoping to hide the fact that the communists had destroyed most Buddhist temples in the country. It worked. After the visit, Gandan became the showcase for foreign visitors. In 1990, it was reopened as a true monastery with religious services. Today, about five hundred monks live and worship at Gandan.

Gandan is open to visitors. The monastery complex includes beautifully maintained temples, artwork, and sculpture.

Mongolian Muslims pray together in a ger. Most Mongolian Muslims are from the Khazak ethnic group.

## Other Religions

Atheism is the belief that there is no God or gods. When communism took hold of Mongolia in the 1920s, the new communist government outlawed religion and replaced it with atheism. Over the years, many Mongolians embraced atheism. Today, a great many Mongolians continue to identify themselves as atheists.

A small but growing number of Mongolians practice Islam. This religion was founded by Muhammad in the 600s. Followers of Islam, called Muslims, believe that God sent messages to Muhammad. These messages were collected in the Qur'an, the Muslim holy book. Most Mongolian Muslims are part of the Kazakh ethnic group who live mainly in Ölgii.

**Mongolian Religious Beliefs**

| | |
|---|---|
| Buddhism | 80% |
| Atheism | 10% |
| Islam | 5% |
| Christianity | 5% |

Christian missionaries poured into Mongolia after the fall of communism. Mongolia now has more than 125 churches.

Christianity is also a growing religion in Mongolia. Many missionaries from other countries have traveled to Mongolia to try to convert people to Christianity. They have started churches in several Mongolian cities, including Ulaanbaatar. Christian groups that have built churches in Mongolia include Mormons and Roman Catholics.

## Shamanism

Shamanism has long thrived alongside Buddhism in the Mongolian culture. It has existed in Mongolia since before the time of the khans and continues to be practiced in many areas of Mongolia today. Shamanism is a belief system that is based around a holy figure, or a shaman. Shamans are believed to have special healing powers and access to the spirit world. Shamans can be male or female. Male shamans are called *boo*, and female shamans are *udgan*. As healers, they cure sicknesses and guide the soul of a dead person to the afterlife. Shamans are also believed to be in contact with the spirit world, acting as a go-between for humans and spirits. It is said that shamans communicate with spirits by going into a trance, which can last several hours.

A shaman has special clothing and equipment, including a cloak, a hat, and a drum. The cloak is usually covered with snake figures that hang from the back. It might also have a mirror to reflect evil and to allow the shaman to see spirits. A shaman's hat is usually adorned with antlers and tied with scarves. The drum is usually made of goatskin.

In the 1920s and 1930s, communist leaders tried to destroy shamanism along with Buddhism. It was harder, though, because shamanism did not have temples, books, or other obvious materials of the faith. Many shamans were killed anyway. The religion went underground for many years. But Mongolians continued to hold rituals in secret. Much of the belief system survived by being passed from parents to children. Today, shamanism is enjoying a revival, especially among Buryat and Darkhad Mongolians.

Shamans are said to be able to cure the sick and banish evil spirits. Many Mongolians rely on a mixture of shamanism and Western medicine when they fall ill.

# Ancient Traditions

Mongolian musicians perform wearing lavish outfits.

Iᴺ Mᴏɴɢᴏʟɪᴀ, sᴘᴏʀᴛs ᴀɴᴅ ᴀʀᴛs ᴀʀᴇ ᴇssᴇɴᴛɪᴀʟ ᴘᴀʀᴛs ᴏғ daily life. Even during the long decades of communist rule, Mongolians continued to hold celebrations and competitions that focused on sports. Since the fall of communism, the arts have again flourished. Singing, music, and fine arts have enjoyed a new awakening, as more Mongolians become aware of their rich artistic heritage.

*Opposite:* **Horsemen parade through the streets of Ulaanbaatar in celebration of the eight hundredth anniversary of Genghis Khan uniting the Mongol tribes.**

During the Naadam festival, archers wear a traditional coat called a *deel*.

### The Naadam Festival

The Naadam festival is the largest sporting event in Mongolia. It is also called Eriin Gurwan Naadam, which means "the Three Manly Games." The three-day celebration, which is held in July in locations all over the country, focuses on the traditional Mongolian sports of wrestling, archery, and horse racing.

No one is sure when the festival began, but it probably started in prehistoric times, when horses were first tamed. By 3000 B.C., it was a regular national celebration. The nomadic tribes would gather in midsummer to show off their strength and their skill in shooting and riding. These qualities were essential for survival on the steppes. The tradition of gathering together to compete continued through the centuries, and it remains a vital part of Mongolian culture. Until recently, only men could participate in the Naadam. Today, women also compete in archery and horseback riding.

Each Naadam festival begins with a parade of athletes and soldiers marching to the music of military bands. Riders dressed in medieval Mongolian armor and toting ancient weapons carry banners representing Genghis Khan. After this ceremony, the games begin. The first two days are filled with competitions. The third day is reserved for feasting and celebration.

**The largest Naadam festival is held every year in Ulaanbaatar. It begins with a grand parade of horsemen.**

The wrestling tournament is the highlight of the Naadam. In the national Naadam in Ulaanbaatar, 512 wrestlers compete. They all enter an arena at the start of the tournament and divide into two groups on either side of the arena. After songs and statements praising the wrestlers and their qualities, the wrestlers are paired for the first match.

The rules of Mongolian wrestling are simple: the first person who hits the ground loses. When the signal is given, the wrestlers rush in to battle their opponents. There are no weight classes, so a very large wrestler might be paired with a very small one. There are no rules for how long a match will

**Mongolian wrestlers wear short jackets and large leather boots. Matches are usually held in a field.**

## Sumo Champion

Many Mongolians have become interested in sumo wrestling in recent years. Sumo wrestling originated in Japan, and most of the world sumo champions are Japanese. Japanese sumo rules allow only forty foreign wrestlers to compete. Of those, twenty-five are Mongolians. One of the greatest Mongolian sumo wrestling champions, Asashoryu D. Dagvadorj, is one of them.

Wrestling came naturally to Dagvadorj. He was born in Ulaanbaatar in 1980 into a family of Mongolian wrestlers. His father and two brothers hold Naadam wrestling titles. When Dagvadorj was still a teenager, he began competing in Japanese sumo wrestling. He competed in fourteen tournaments in his first two years as a professional wrestler. He quickly became known for his skill, achieving the rank of Komusubi, the fourth-highest rank in sumo wrestling—an impressive achievement for a young wrestler from Mongolia.

In 2005, Dagvadorj won the title of grand champion for the seventh time, becoming the first wrestler of any country to win that many tournaments in a row. His stunning victory earned him the nickname "Pride of Mongolia."

last. Some matches last as long as two hours, as two wrestlers stay locked together.

The winners go on to the second round, where they are divided into two groups again and paired for their next match. The tournament lasts for two days and eight matches. Winners of a certain number of rounds receive titles. Those who win five rounds are called Falcons. Winners of seven rounds are given the title of Elephant. By the end of the second day, only the strongest wrestlers are left. The final wrestlers battle for the highest honor, the title of Titan.

Archery contests have been held in Mongolia for a thousand years.

## *Archery*

Archery was once a vital skill in Mongolian life. Today, it is a highly respected sport and one of the main Naadam events. Archers compete in teams of five to seven. Their goal is to hit thirty-three leather cylinders that are 246 feet (75 m) away. Women's targets are 197 feet (60 m) away.

Judges, who stand near the targets, judge each shot with a yell, called a *uukhai*, and a raised hand. The winning archer, or *mergen*, is the one who hits the targets the most times.

All contestants wear traditional costumes during the event. They use a special type of bent bow that is made of horn, bark, and wood. Their arrows are made from willow branches and vulture feathers.

## Horse Racing

Horse racing is the third "manly game" of the Naadam. One popular saying goes, "Mongols are born on horseback." Horses are a central part of Mongolian culture, and the horse races reflect that. In fact, during the Naadam, the awards and honors go to the horse, not to its rider or owner.

The approximately one thousand horses that will run the Naadam race are chosen a month before the event. Their owners give them special food and training for the big day. The race is broken down into six categories based on the ages

**Though horse racing is one of the Naadam festival's "manly" sports, children serve as jockeys during the event.**

of the horses. Horses in each age group run a different distance, from 10 miles (16 km) up to 19 miles (30 km). The race is conducted on the open steppe, with no specific track or course. The horse and rider must navigate the land, rivers, hills, and other natural obstacles.

The horses are ridden by children who range in age from about five to twelve years old. Mongolians believe that a small, lightweight rider allows a horse to run its best. Using small children also makes it more likely that the race's winner will be determined by the skill of the horse, not the skill of the rider. The winning horse is awarded the title "Leader of Ten Thousand," and the five runners-up are given medals.

## Tsagaan Sar

The first festival of the year is Tsagaan Sar, the Lunar New Year. It is also the country's largest festival. The holiday falls in January or February. It lasts anywhere from three days to a few weeks, depending on the families involved and where they live in Mongolia. Many of the traditional customs of Tsagaan Sar are centuries old. People wear new, elegant clothing. They clean their homes. On the eve of the holiday, every family prepares a big meal. There is usually a wrestling match broadcast on television that evening. On the steppes, nomads ride their best horses during the holiday.

During Tsagaan Sar, Mongolians visit their relatives, exchange gifts, and eat meals together. Guests are warmly welcomed into the home and are served tea and food. Children get presents and candy.

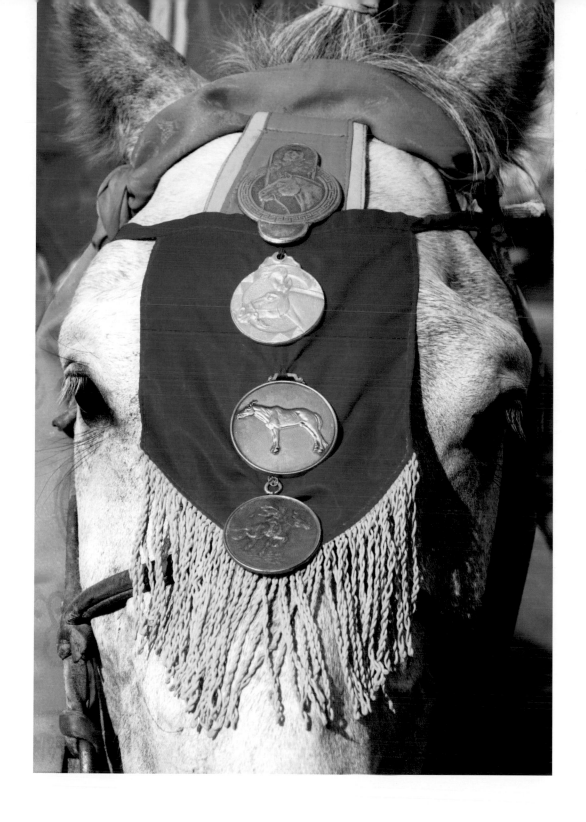

## A Traditional Mongolian Wedding

Traditionally, Mongolian marriages were arranged by the couple's parents, sometimes when the bride and groom were still children. When both the bride and groom were at least eighteen years old, the marriage could finally take place.

The engagement happened in three stages. First, a friend of the groom's family visited the bride's family and proposed the match. If the family was agreeable, then the groom's family visited the bride's family and offered gifts. If those were accepted, the couple was considered to be engaged. The third stage occurred when the groom delivered gifts to his bride's family himself.

On the day of the wedding, the bride and groom wore new, brightly colored versions of their ordinary clothing. A typical color for a bride's outfit was red, green, or blue. The groom and his party rode on horseback to the bride's house for a huge feast. Then they took the bride and her party back to the groom's house, where she was given special jewelry signifying that she was now a married woman. After prayers and blessings, the couple were considered married.

Today, Mongolians don't usually observe such complex wedding customs. Most Mongolian brides wear Western-style white bridal gowns, and the grooms usually wear suits or tuxedos. The families still exchange gifts, however.

## The Arts

Mongolia enjoyed a strong artistic tradition until the rise of communism in the 1920s. Because many of the artistic styles expressed Buddhist religious beliefs, the communist government considered them religious and therefore illegal. Many traditional arts were abandoned or practiced in secret. Instead, the communist government supported arts such as ballet and theater.

With the political changes of the early 1990s, the communist-sponsored arts groups in Mongolia were no longer funded, so many of them closed. At the same time, people gained a new appreciation for traditional Mongolian arts. Today, Mongolians have the freedom to express themselves through art.

## Mongolian Museums

Zanabazar Museum of Fine Arts in Ulaanbaatar was founded in 1966. The museum houses more than ten thousand sculptures, paintings, and other objects. Most were made by Mongolian artists who lived in the early twentieth century or before. Among the museum's best-known sculptures are works by Zanabazar, the first spiritual head of Tibetan Buddhism in Mongolia. The museum also exhibits old, rare scroll paintings; Buddhist statues; and *tsam* masks, which are worn by monks during religious ceremonies.

The National Museum of Mongolian History, which was founded in 1991, focuses on the history and culture of Mongols from ancient to modern times. Among the fifteen thousand items on display are several objects from the Hun period, dating back two thousand years. These include a Mongolian soldier's leather boots, carpets, and silk goods. Also on display are Mongolian costumes and jewelry, Mongolian armor, a complete furnished ger, and musical instruments.

The Winter Palace of Bogd Khan was one of the first museums in Mongolia. Built between 1893 and 1903, it was the winter home of the last figurehead of Buddhism in Mongolia, Bogd Khan, who was also the country's emperor. The palace is known for its Gate of Peace, its temple, and the Bogd Khan's personal library. The communist government turned the palace into a museum in 1924. It is not known why the communists did not destroy it.

## Music

Vocal music has a long, rich history in Mongolian culture. Music is part of the lives of the nomads, and singing voices often drift out over the vast landscape. It is normal to hear Mongolians singing during the birth of a calf, as they work with their herds, or at the breathtaking beauty of white clouds against a deep blue sky.

In years past, Mongolian tribes would come together to share food and news, and they would also share their music. In this way, much of the country's musical tradition was preserved for centuries. Mongolians sing two types of songs, "short" songs and "long" songs. Short songs are sung with great expression and gestures, and they only last a few min-

**Music is an everyday part of Mongolian life. Now, traditional Mongolian music is also performed for audiences.**

No one knows when throat singing began. Some people say it got its start when herders tried to duplicate sounds they heard in nature, such as the whistling wind or bubbling water.

utes. Long songs are sung unemotionally, and they last for quite a while. Songs can be about any number of things: stories of ancient heroes, the kindness of family, a mother's love, or the beauty of the world.

Northwestern Mongolia is one of the few places in the world where a rare type of singing called "throat singing" is performed. In this unusual, often droning music, the singer actually produces two different pitches at the same time.

## The Horse-Head Fiddle

The *morin khuur,* or horse-head fiddle, is one of the oldest traditional Mongolian instruments. It is named for the beautiful carving of a horse's head that appears on the scroll of the instrument. The fiddle is a two-stringed box instrument that usually accompanies singing. The instrument is so respected that it is placed in the rear section of the ger, the most honored part of the hut.

During the communist era, Mongolia's tradition of singing suffered greatly. In the 1920s, the words to many songs were rewritten to glorify the communist government and its heroes. Songs with Buddhist or other religious themes were banned. A great deal of music disappeared or was forgotten. Today, the government is working with the United Nations Educational, Scientific, and Cultural Organization (UNESCO) to save the songs of the Mongolian nomads. The plan is to create a fund to pay for recording this music and preserving the traditional songs of the steppes. Several musical groups, including the Tumen Ekh Ensemble, now perform this traditional Mongolian music around the world.

## Tangkas

Until recently, few Mongolians had ever heard about one of the country's most beautiful traditional art forms, the *tangkas*. Tangkas are enormous fabric banners decorated with pictures and symbols. One tangka could be up to 52 feet (16 m) long and 36 feet (11 m) wide. It took teams of women several months to make one tangka. Some elaborate tangkas were decorated with gold thread, silver, and precious stones, and only the wealthiest monasteries could afford these.

Tangkas were made for a Buddhist ceremony of wealth and protection. On the day of the ceremony, monks would march through Ulaanbaatar, chanting prayers and carrying the magnificent banners on long poles. The images on colorful tangkas included gods and symbols that stood for eternity, long life, good health, and happiness. At the end of the march, there would be a tsam-mask dance, a ceremony that acted out a battle between good and bad spirits.

The last tsam dance was performed in the 1930s.

When the communists destroyed the Buddhist temples, they destroyed most of these gorgeous banners as well. Tangkas were banned and forgotten. But a few were saved and hidden away. Some were stored in the cellars of the Mongolian Fine Arts Museum. Today, several of these fragile textiles are being slowly restored to their former beauty.

</</k>

CHAPTER

TEN

# Life Under the Bright Blue Sky

At THE BEGINNING OF THE TWENTIETH CENTURY, only about five hundred thousand people lived in Mongolia. During the communist years, the population soared. This was mainly because of improved education and health care under the communist system. Today, about 2.8 million people live in Mongolia. Seventy percent of the population is under thirty-five years old.

*Opposite:* **A young girl leans on a motorcycle on the Mongolian grasslands.**

**About 32 percent of Mongolians are under age fourteen.**

The lives of Mongolian city dwellers are vastly different from those of nomads who live on the steppes. Mongolians who live in Ulaanbaatar enjoy the same lifestyle as anyone else who lives in a big city. They have office jobs and live in apartments. Some can afford to go out to the theater or a restaurant.

The lives of Mongolian nomads are in rhythm with the natural world. They live in gers and move their herds across the steppes with the seasons. For all Mongolians, certain aspects of daily life are the same.

The State Department Store is the largest store in Mongolia. At the store, shoppers can buy books, clothes, souvenirs, and much more.

Almost all Mongolians can read and write.

## School

Mongolia boasts a 98 percent literacy rate, one of the highest rates in the world. Education thrived under communist rule in Mongolia. The communist government opened schools throughout Mongolia, and children were required to attend. Today, more than half a million Mongolians attend school.

Every child in Mongolia is required to attend primary school, which lasts four years. After that, children attend secondary school, which lasts six years. Mongolia currently has 232 ten-year schools that combine primary and secondary classes. Primary students learn the Mongolian language, mathematics, history and social studies, natural sciences, music, and art.

### Mongolian Holidays

| | |
|---|---|
| Shin Jil (New Year's Day) | January 1 |
| Constitution Day | January 13 |
| Tsagaan Sar (Lunar New Year) | January/February |
| Women's Day | March 8 |
| Mother and Children's Day | June 1 |
| Naadam | July 11–13 |
| Mongolian Republic Day | November 26 |

Students work on an engine at a vocational training center in Ulaanbaatar. About twenty thousand students attend vocational schools in Mongolia.

Secondary school is divided into lower secondary and higher secondary. Children aged twelve to sixteen go to lower secondary. Upper secondary is for students aged seventeen to eighteen. All secondary students study the Mongolian language, Mongolian literature, foreign languages (usually English and Russian), mathematics, natural sciences, geography, biology, physics, chemistry, astronomy, history and social studies, music, physical education, and art.

### Ice Shagai Game

The traditional Mongolian game of ice *shagai* is simple but challenging. It is played in winter, on the ice of a frozen river or lake. Players clear a patch of ice and place five sheep anklebones between two stones. The goal is to slide a ball down the ice and hit as many anklebones as possible.

Ice shagai was first mentioned in a medieval Mongolian document called *The Secret History of the Mongols*. It says that Genghis Khan played this game. In the 1950s, the game was so popular that a national championship was held each year. Today, the game is enjoying new popularity. It is not unusual to see several groups of players gathered along a frozen river in the winter, testing their skill.

After secondary school, students have several choices. They can go to a technical or trade school, or they can attend a university or college. Most students attend college in Mongolia, but many dream of attending college in countries such as Germany, the United States, and Japan.

**Children play on a frozen stream in northern Mongolia. Winter lasts six months in this part of Mongolia.**

## Food

Most Mongolian food is based on the diet of the nomads—lots of meat and dairy products. Most foods are hearty but somewhat bland. The traditional Mongolian diet didn't include breads or fresh vegetables. The main reason for this is that nomads did not plant or harvest crops, or transport ovens for baking. Instead, Mongolian nomads relied on the foods they could get from their herds.

Food in Mongolia is dependent on the seasons. Livestock produce the most milk in the summer months, so dairy products such as cheese are the main summer foods. Meat is the main food for the winter months. Mongolians sometimes

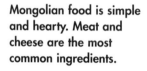
Mongolian food is simple and hearty. Meat and cheese are the most common ingredients.

Mongolians cook in big metal bowls. A stove in the middle of the ger both cooks the food and heats the home.

add potatoes to their diet. Recently, they have begun enjoying more fresh vegetables, foods made with flour or rice, and processed foods. Today, most Mongolian meals include some kind of bread and a dish called *shuulte khool*, which is a soup of broth, pasta, boiled meat, and sometimes potatoes.

Other traditional Mongolian foods include *buuz* (steamed mutton dumplings) and *khuushuur* (fried pancakes made with mutton). These dishes are made by local families on the steppes. They are also served in restaurants.

The most common food of the nomads is *makh*, or meat. Mongolians cook meat by boiling meat bones, fat, and some animal organs in a big metal bowl. Nomads also eat dried meat. They enjoy a souplike dish called *khorkhog*, which is made by putting hot stones into a pot with mutton, water, salt, onions, and other spices.

In the summer, Mongolians eat a great deal of *tsagaan idee*, which means "white food." Tsagaan idee are made from dairy products, which give them their name. Milk is stirred and

### Airag, the Mongolian Drink

No Mongolian celebration is complete without a drink of *airag*. This mild drink is made from fermented horse's milk. Airag is very good for quenching thirst, and it is a staple of the Mongolian diet.

Airag is made during the summer in a special bag made of skin. Fresh horse's milk is poured into the skin, along with other ingredients to make it ferment properly. The mix is stirred regularly with a wooden stick. Every person who enters or leaves the ger stirs the milk as they pass by. The longer the liquid is allowed to ferment, the stronger it will become.

boiled for several hours and then allowed to cool. The *urum*, or skin, that forms on the boiled milk is removed. The boiled milk is used to make yogurt and a dry, sweet curd called *aaruul*. Other white foods include a cheese called *byaslag* and a food similar to cheese called *eedem*. *Khoormog* is yogurt made from camel's milk. Mongolian nomads also enjoy a soft fermented cheese called *aarts*.

Tea is the main drink of the Mongolian people. Most people insist on a cup of tea before every meal. A typical tea drink is *süütei tsai*, which is milk tea with salt. In some areas, they add fresh butter to their tea.

### Housing

Mongolia's traditional hut, the ger, is still widely used throughout the country. Although it is mainly a home for nomads since it can be easily transported, ger villages are common in or near large cities.

Gers are surprisingly comfortable and roomy. They are well suited to life on the steppes. A ger's round shape gives it strength against strong winds. It is protected by a double layer of thick felt, which keeps it warm during the winter. Most gers have a wooden door that is beautifully painted or decorated. Red is the usual color for a ger door.

Inside a ger, the fireplace or stove is in the center. The kitchen area is on the eastern side of the stove. Beds are arranged along the sides of the ger, with the master of the

Every ger has a stove in the center. Smoke from the fire is vented out through a hole in the ceiling.

house sleeping on the northeast side. The area opposite the door is considered an honorable or sacred spot in the ger. Special possessions, religious items, and other sacred objects are stored there.

In the cities, most Mongolians live in boxy apartment buildings that were built during Mongolia's communist years.

## Clothing

Most Mongolians dress in Western clothing such as pants, dresses, and shirts. Traditional Mongolian clothing is seen more in rural areas. Even there, it is mainly worn during festivals or celebrations.

The most common Mongolian garment is the *deel,* a general word for "coat" in the Mongolian language. Both men and women wear deels, which can be made with either ordinary fabrics or expensive silks and brocades. A deel is held together with a decorative belt. Many people wear traditional Mongolian costumes during the Naadam competitions. The archers, in particular, compete while wearing brightly colored deels and fur-lined hats.

## The Appeal of the Steppes

The Mongolian people have survived, and they have thrived. The nomadic way of life that was common in the days of Marco Polo is still very much a part of Mongolian culture. Every season, thousands of herders break down their gers and move their livestock across the fenceless steppes, just as they did in the time of the great khans. Even city dwellers have

felt the pull of the nomadic life. Some have left the city and started herds of their own. It is a hard life, but an independent one. On the steppes, there is no one to tell you what to do. For many Mongolian families, this is the only way to live.

**Mongolian horses are small and tough. Able to trot all day through the wind and cold, they are the perfect horses for the steppes.**

# Timeline

| Mongolian History | | World History | |
|---|---|---|---|
| Earliest evidence of humans in Mongolia. | 100,000–200,000 years ago | | |
| Chinese writers first describe the Mongol tribes. | 5th–4th century B.C. | | |
| | | 2500 B.C. | Egyptians build the pyramids and the Sphinx in Giza. |
| | | 563 B.C. | The Buddha is born in India. |
| | | A.D. 313 | The Roman emperor Constantine legalizes Christianity. |
| | | 610 | The Prophet Muhammad begins preaching a new religion called Islam. |
| | | 1054 | The Eastern (Orthodox) and Western (Roman Catholic) Churches break apart. |
| | | 1095 | The Crusades begin. |
| Genghis Khan is born. | 1162 or 1167 | | |
| Genghis Khan's army sacks Yanjing (Beijing). | 1215 | 1215 | King John seals the Magna Carta. |
| Genghis Khan dies. | 1227 | | |
| Mongol armies invade Europe. | 1240–1241 | | |
| Khublai, the grandson of Genghis, becomes khan. | 1260 | | |
| Marco Polo visits Mongolia. | 1275 | | |
| Khublai Khan dies; tribal war and infighting weaken the Mongols. | 1294 | | |
| The Mongols are expelled from Beijing. | 1368 | | |
| | | 1300s | The Renaissance begins in Italy. |
| | | 1347 | The plague sweeps through Europe. |
| | | 1453 | Ottoman Turks capture Constantinople, conquering the Byzantine Empire. |
| | | 1492 | Columbus arrives in North America. |
| | | 1500s | Reformers break away from the Catholic Church, and Protestantism is born. |

| Mongolian History | | World History | |
|---|---|---|---|
| Zanabazar is recognized as the first spiritual head of Buddhism in Mongolia. | 1639 | | |
| The Qing dynasty in China conquers the southern Mongols. | 1691 | | |
| The Treaty of Kyakhta creates the border between Russia and Mongolia. | 1727 | | |
| | | 1776 | The Declaration of Independence is signed. |
| | | 1789 | The French Revolution begins. |
| | | 1865 | The American Civil War ends. |
| | | 1879 | The first practical light bulb is invented. |
| The Qing dynasty falls; Mongolia declares its independence. | 1911 | | |
| | | 1914 | World War I breaks out. |
| | | 1917 | The Bolshevik Revolution brings communism to Russia. |
| Communism takes hold in Mongolia. | 1920s | | |
| Buddhism is intentionally destroyed in Mongolia; thousands of monks are murdered. | 1920s–1930s | 1929 | A worldwide economic depression begins. |
| | | 1939 | World War II begins. |
| | | 1945 | World War II ends. |
| | | 1957 | The Vietnam War starts. |
| | | 1969 | Humans land on the Moon. |
| | | 1975 | The Vietnam War ends. |
| | | 1989 | The Berlin Wall is torn down as communism crumbles in Eastern Europe. |
| Communism ends in Mongolia. | 1990 | | |
| Mongolia's new constitution, which emphasizes human rights, goes into effect. | 1992 | 1991 | The Soviet Union breaks into separate states. |
| | | 2001 | Terrorists attack the World Trade Center, New York, and the Pentagon, Washington, D.C. |
| The government headed by Tsakhiagiin Elbegdorj is overthrown. | 2006 | | |

# Fast Facts

**Official name:** Mongolia

**Capital:** Ulaanbaatar

**Official language:** Mongolian

Ulaanbaatar

Mongolia's flag

| | |
|---|---|
| **Official religion:** | None |
| **National anthem:** | "National Anthem of Mongolia" |
| **Government:** | Multiparty parliamentary democracy |
| **Chief of state:** | President |
| **Head of government:** | Prime minister |
| **Area:** | 603,909 square miles (1,564,116 sq km) |
| **Latitude and longitude of Ulaanbaatar:** | 47°54'N, 106° 52'E |
| **Bordering countries:** | China, Russia |
| **Highest elevation:** | Nairamdliin Orgil, 14,350 feet (4,374 m) |
| **Lowest elevation:** | Khokh Nuur, 1,699 feet (518 m) |
| **Average high temperature in Ulaanbaatar:** | January 2°F (-19°C)<br>July 72°F (22°C) |
| **Average annual precipitation:** | 8–9 inches (20–22 cm) |
| **National population (2006 est.):** | 2,832,224 |

Khövsgöl Nuur

Gandan Khiid

Currency

**Population of largest cities:**

| | |
|---|---|
| Ulaanbaatar | 850,000 |
| Erdenet | 68,310 |
| Darkhan | 65,791 |
| Choibalsan | 41,000 |

**Famous landmarks:**
- ▶ *Gandan Khiid,* Ulaanbaatar
- ▶ *National Museum of Mongolian History,* Ulaanbaatar
- ▶ *Khustai National Park,* Khentii Nuruu range

**Industry:** Mongolia's primary industry is agriculture and livestock. The main livestock raised are horses, camels, cattle, goats, sheep, and camels. Mining has been growing in recent years, but manufacturing plays only a small part in the economy.

**Currency:** Mongolia's currency is called the togrog or tugrik. About 1,120 togrogs equaled 1 U.S. dollar in 2006.

**System of weights and measures:** Metric system

**Literacy (2004):** 98%

Schoolchildren

**Common Mongolian words and phrases:**

| | |
|---|---|
| *Sain baina uu* | Hello |
| *Bayartai* | Good-bye |
| *Tiim* | Yes |
| *Ügüi* | No |
| *Bayarlaa* | Thanks |
| *Uuchlaarai* | Excuse me |
| *Tany neriig khen gedeg ve* | What is your name? |
| *Minii neriig . . .* | My name is . . . |
| *Sonin salkhan yu baina?* | What's new? |
| *To kheden nastai ve?* | How old are you? |
| *Bid airag uukh gesen yum* | We'd like to drink some airag. |

Asashoryu D. Dagvadorj

**Famous Mongolians:**

Asashoryu D. Dagvadorj (1980– )
*Sumo wrestler*

Genghis Khan (1162 or 1167–1227)
*Creator of the Mongol empire*

Hulegu Khan (1217–1265)
*Leader who conquered much of southwest Asia*

Khublai Khan (1215–1294)
*Ruler who conquered most of China*

Damdin Sükhbaatar (1893–1923)
*Military hero*

Zanabazar (1635–1723)
*Religious leader*

# To Find Out More

## Books

▶ Guek-Cheng Pang. *Mongolia*. Cultures of the World. London: Marshall Cavendish Publications, 1999.

▶ Hanson, Jennifer. *Mongolia*. Nations in Transition. New York: Facts on File, 2003.

▶ Kohn, Michael. *Mongolia*. Victoria, Australia: Lonely Planet Publications, 2005.

▶ Taylor, Robert. *Life in Genghis Khan's Mongolia*. San Diego, Calif.: Lucent Books, 2000.

## Web Sites

▶ **Lonely Planet Mongolia** www.lonelyplanet.com/worldguide/ destinations/asia/mongolia *A basic travel guide to Mongolia.*

▶ **Mongolia Today** www.mongoliatoday.com *An online magazine with articles on Mongolian culture and history along with practical information for visitors.*

▶ **The World Factbook: Mongolia** www.cia.gov/cia/publications/ factbook/geos/mg.html *For up-to-date statistics and general information about Mongolia.*

## Organizations and Embassies

▶ **Embassy of Mongolia**
2833 M Street NW
Washington, DC 20007
202-333-7117

▶ **Embassy of Mongolia**
151 Slater Street
Suite 103
Ottawa, Ontario K1P 5H3
613-569-3830

▶ **Permanent Mission of Mongolia
to the United Nations**
6 East 77th Street
New York, NY 10021
212-861-9460

# Index

Page numbers in *italics* indicate illustrations.

# Meet the Author

Allison Lassieur is a writer living in Trenton, Tennessee. She has written more than eighty books for children and young adults, on subjects including history, current events, science, animals, famous people, and countries. Allison also writes magazine articles, short stories, and materials for game and toy companies. When she isn't writing, she loves to take long walks with her dogs and spend time with her family.

Researching this book was a challenge. For many years, during the communist rule of Mongolia, little information was known or published outside the country. The changes that

have come to Mongolia in recent years have been so swift that books just a few years old are already hopelessly out-of-date. So Allison had to get creative with her research. She talked to people who had visited Mongolia since 1990. She dug up a few hard-to-find academic books that were written since the end of communism in Mongolia. She found Web sites with current information and news about the country. She even made a *deel* to see what it feels like to wear traditional Mongolian clothing. She made one for her husband, too.

Now, when someone asks Allison if she'd like to go to Mongolia, she answers with an enthusiastic "Yes!"

# Photo Credits